Monologues from Shakespeare's First Folio for Women:
The Histories

The Applause Shakespeare Monologue Series

Other Shakespeare Titles From Applause

Once More unto the Speech Dear Friends
Volume One: The Comedies
Compiled and Edited with Commentary by Neil Freeman

Once More unto the Speech Dear Friends
Volume Two: The Histories
Compiled and Edited with Commentary by Neil Freeman

Once More unto the Speech Dear Friends
Volume Three: The Tragedies
Compiled and Edited with Commentary by Neil Freeman

The Applause First Folio in Modern Type
Prepared and Annotated by Neil Freeman

The Folio Texts
Prepared and Annotated by Neil Freeman, Each of the 36 plays of the
Applause First Folio in Modern Type individually bound

The Applause Shakespeare Library
Plays of Shakespeare Edited for Performance

Soliloquy: The Shakespeare Monologues

Monologues from Shakespeare's First Folio for Women:
The Histories

Compilation and Commentary by
Neil Freeman

Edited by
Paul Sugarman

APPLAUSE
THEATRE & CINEMA BOOKS
Guilford, Connecticut

APPLAUSE
THEATRE & CINEMA BOOKS

An imprint of Globe Pequot, the trade division of
The Rowman & Littlefield Publishing Group, Inc.
4501 Forbes Blvd., Ste. 200
Lanham, MD 20706
www.rowman.com

Distributed by NATIONAL BOOK NETWORK

Material drawn from *Once More Unto the Speech Dear Friends*
Copyright © 2006 Folio Scripts, Vancouver Canada. Published by Applause Theatre
& Cinema Books in 2006.

Library of Congress Cataloging-in-Publication Data available

Library of Congress Control Number: 2021944384

ISBN 978-1-4930-5684-2 (paperback)
ISBN 978-1-4930-5685-9 (ebook)

Dedication

Although Neil Freeman passed to that "undiscovered country" in 2015, his work continues to lead students and actors to a deeper understanding of Shakespeare's plays. With the exception of Shakespeare's words (and my humble foreword), the entirety of the material within these pages is Neil's. May these editions serve as a lasting legacy to a life of dedicated scholarship, and a great passion for Shakespeare.

Contents

FOREWORD

Paul Sugarman

Monologues from Shakespeare's First Folio presents the work of Neil Freeman, longtime champion of Shakespeare's First Folio, whose groundbreaking explorations into how first printings offered insights to the text in rehearsals, stage and in the classroom. This work continued with *Once More Unto the Speech Dear Friends: Monologues from Shakespeare's First Folio with Modern Text Versions for Comparison* where Neil collected over 900 monologues divided between the Comedy, History and Tragedy Published by Applause in three masterful volumes which present the original First Folio text side by side with the modern, edited version of the text. These volumes provide a massive amount of material and information. However both the literary scope, and the literal size of these volumes can be intimidating and overwhelming. This series' intent is to make the work more accessible by taking material from the encyclopediac original volumes and presenting it in an accessible workbook format.

To better focus the work for actors and students the texts are contrasted side by side with introductory notes before and commentary after to aid the exploration of the text. By comparing modern and First Folio printings, Neil points the way to gain new insights into Shakespeare's text. Editors over the centuries have "corrected" and updated the texts to make them "accessible," or "grammatically correct." In doing so they have lost vital clues and information that Shakespeare placed there for his actors. With the texts side by side, you can see where and why editors have made changes and what may have been lost in translation.

In addition to being divided into Histories, Comedies, and Tragedies, the original series further breaks down speeches by the character's designated gender, also indicating speeches appropriate for any gender. Drawing from this example, this series breaks down each original volume into four workbooks: speeches for Women of all ages, Younger Men, Older Men and Any Gender. Gender is naturally fluid for Shakespeare's characters since during his time, ALL of the characters were portrayed by males. Contemporary productions of Shakespeare commonly switch character genders (Prospero has become Prospera), in addition to presenting single gender, reverse gender and gender non-specific productions. There are certainly characters and speeches where the gender is immaterial, hence the inclusion of a volume of speeches for Any Gender. This was something that Neil had indicated in the original volumes; we are merely following his example.

The monologues in the book are arranged by play in approximate order of composition, so you get his earliest plays first and can observe how his rhetorical art developed over time. The speeches are then arranged by their order in the play.

Once More Unto the Speech Dear Friends was a culmination of Neil's dedicated efforts to make the First Folio more accessible and available to readers and to illuminate for actors the many clues within the Folio text, as originally published. The material in this book is drawn from that work and retains Neil's British spelling of words (i.e. capitalisation) and his extensive commentary on each speech. Neil went on to continue this work as a master teacher of Shakespeare with another series of Shakespeare editions, his 'rhythm texts' and the ebook that he published on Apple Books, *The Shakespeare Variations.*

Neil published on his own First Folio editions of the plays in modern type which were the basis the Folio Texts series published by Applause of all 36 plays in the First Folio. These individual editions all have extensive notes on the changes that modern editions had made. This material was then combined to create a complete reproduction of the First Folio in modern type, *The Applause First Folio of Shakespeare in Modern Type.* These editions make the First Folio more accessible than ever before. The examples in this book demonstrate how the clues from the First Folio will give insights to understanding and performing these speeches and why it is a worthwhile endeavour to discover the riches in the First Folio.

PREFACE AND BRIEF BACKGROUND TO THE FIRST FOLIO

There has been an enormous change in theatre organisation recent in the last twenty years. While the major large-scale companies have continued to flourish, many small theatre companies have come into being, leading to

- much doubling
- cross gender casting, with many one time male roles now being played legitimately by/as women in updated time-period productions
- young actors being asked to play leading roles at far earlier points in their careers

All this has meant actors should be able to demonstrate enormous flexibility rather than one limited range/style. In turn, this has meant

- a change in audition expectations
- actors are often expected to show more range than ever before
- often several shorter audition speeches are asked for instead of one or two longer ones
- sometimes the initial auditions are conducted in a shorter amount of time

Thus, to stay at the top of the game, the actor needs more knowledge of what makes the play tick, especially since

- early plays demand a different style from the later ones
- the four genres (comedy, history, tragedy, and the peculiar romances) all have different acting/textual requirements
- parts originally written for the older, more experienced actors again require a different approach from those written for the younger

ones, as the young roles, especially the female ones, were played by young actors extraordinarily skilled in the arts of rhetoric

There's now much more knowledge of how the original quarto and folio texts can add to the rehearsal exploration/acting and directing process as well as to the final performance.

Each speech is made up of four parts

- a background to the speech, placing it in the context of the play, and offering line length and an approximate timing to help you choose what might be right for any auditioning occasion
- a modern text version of the speech, with the sentence structure clearly delineated side by side with
- a folio version of the speech, where modern texts changes to the capitalization, spelling and sentence structure can be plainly seen
- a commentary explaining the differences between the two texts, and in what way the original setting can offer you more information to explore

Thus if they wish, **beginners** can explore just the background and the modern text version of the speech.

An actor experienced in exploring the Folio can make use of the background and the Folio version of the speech

And those wanting to know as many details as possible and how they could help define the deft stepping stones of the arc of the speech can use all four elements on the page.

The First Folio

(FOR LIST OF CURRENT REPRODUCTIONS SEE BIBLIOGRAPHY

The end of 1623 saw the publication of the justifiably famed First Folio (F1). The single volume, published in a run of approximately 1,000 copies at the princely sum of one pound (a tremendous risk, considering that a single play would sell at no more than six pence, one fortieth of F1's price, and that the annual salary of a schoolmaster was only ten pounds), contained thirty-six plays.

The manuscripts from which each F1 play would be printed came from a variety of sources. Some had already been printed. Some came from the playhouse complete with production details. Some had no theatrical input at all, but were handsomely copied out and easy to read. Some were supposedly very messy, complete with first draft scribbles and crossings out. Yet, as Charlton Hinman, the revered dean of First Folio studies describes F1 in the Introduction to the Norton Facsimile:

> It is of inestimable value for what it is, for what it contains. For here are preserved the masterworks of the man universally recognized as our greatest writer; and preserved, as Ben Jonson realized at the time of the original publication, not for an age but for all time.

WHAT DOES F1 REPRESENT?

- texts prepared for actors who rehearsed three days for a new play and one day for one already in the repertoire
- written in a style (rhetoric incorporating debate) so different from ours (grammatical) that many modern alterations based on grammar (or poetry) have done remarkable harm to the rhetorical/debate quality of the original text and thus to interpretations of characters at key moments of stress.
- written for an acting company the core of which steadily grew older, and whose skills and interests changed markedly over twenty years as well as for an audience whose make-up and interests likewise changed as the company grew more experienced

The whole is based upon supposedly the best documents available at the time, collected by men closest to Shakespeare throughout his career, and brought to a single printing house whose errors are now widely understood - far more than those of some of the printing houses that produced the original quartos.

TEXTUAL SOURCES FOR THE AUDITION SPEECHES

Individual modern editions consulted in the preparation of the Modern Text version of the speeches are listed in the Bibliography under the separate headings 'The Complete Works in Compendium Format' and ' The Complete Works in Separate Individual Volumes.' Most of the modern versions of the speeches are a compilation of several of these texts. However, all modern act, scene and/or line numbers refer the reader to The Riverside Shakespeare, in my opinion still the best of the complete works despite the excellent compendiums that have been published since.

The First Folio versions of the speeches are taken from a variety of already published sources, including not only all the texts listed in the 'Photostatted Reproductions in Compendium Format' section of the Bibliography, but also earlier, individually printed volumes, such as the twentieth century editions published under the collective title *The Facsimiles of Plays from The First Folio of Shakespeare* by Faber & Gwyer, and the nineteenth century editions published on behalf of The New Shakespeare Society.

INTRODUCTION

So, congratulations , you've got an audition, and for a Shakespeare play no less.

You've done all your homework, including, hopefully , reading the whole play to see the full range and development of the character.

You've got an idea of the character, the situation in which you/it finds itself (the given circumstance s); what your/its needs are (objectives/ intentions); and what you intend to do about them (action /tactics).

You've looked up all the unusual words in a good dictionary or glos- sary; you've turned to a well edited modern edition to find out what some of the more obscure references mean.

And those of you who understand metre and rhythm have worked on the poetic values of the speech, and you are word perfect . . .

. . . and yet it's still not working properly and/or you feel there's more to be gleaned from the text , but you're not sure what that something is or how to go about getting at it; in other words, all is not quite right, yet.

THE KEY QUESTION
What text have you been working with - a good modern text or an 'original' text, that is a copy of one of the first printings of the play?

If it's a modern text, no matter how well edited (and there are some splendid single copy editions available, see the Bibliography for further details), despite all the learned information offered, it's not surpris- ing you feel somewhat at a loss, for there is a huge difference between the original printings (the First Folio, and the individual quartos, see

Appendix 1 for further details) and any text prepared after 1700 right up to the most modern of editions. All the post 1700 texts have been tidied-up for the modern reader to ingest silently, revamped according to the rules of correct grammar, syntax and poetry. However the 'originals' were prepared for actors speaking aloud playing characters often in a great deal of emotional and/or intellectual stress, and were set down on paper according to the very flexible rules of rhetoric and a seemingly very cavalier attitude towards the rules of grammar, and syntax, and spelling, and capitalisation, and even poetry.

Unfortunately, because of the grammatical and syntactical standardisation in place by the early 1700's, many of the quirks and oddities of the origin also have been dismissed as 'accidental' - usually as compositor error either in deciphering the original manuscript, falling prey to their own particular idosyncracies, or not having calculated correctly the amount of space needed to set the text. Modern texts dismiss the possibility that these very quirks and oddities may be by Shakespeare, hearing his characters in as much difficulty as poor Peter Quince is in *A Midsummer Night's Dream* (when he, as the Prologue, terrified and struck down by stage fright, makes a huge grammatical hash in introducing his play 'Pyramus and Thisbe' before the aristocracy, whose acceptance or otherwise, can make or break him)

> If we offend, it is with our good will.
> That you should think, we come not to offend,
> But with good will.
> > To show our simple skill,
> That is the true beginning of our end .
> Consider then, we come but in despite.
> We do not come, as minding to content you ,
> Our true intent is.
> > All for your delight
> We are not here.
> > That you should here repent you,

The Actors are at hand; and by their show,
You shall know all, that you are like to know.

(A Midsummer Night's Dream)

In many other cases in the complete works what was originally printed is equally 'peculiar,' but, unlike Peter Quince , these peculiarities are usually regularised by most modern texts.

However, this series of volumes is based on the belief - as the following will show - that most of these 'peculiarities' resulted from Shakespeare setting down for his actors the stresses, trials, and tribulations the characters are experiencing as they think and speak, and thus are theatrical gold-dust for the actor, director, scholar, teacher, and general reader alike.

THE FIRST ESSENTIAL DIFFERENCE BETWEEN THE TWO TEXTS

THINKING

A **modern** text can show

- the story line
- your character's conflict with the world at large
- your character's conflict with certain individuals within that world

but because of the very way an 'original' text was set, it can show you all this plus one key extra, the very thing that makes big speeches what they are

- the conflict within the character

WHY?

Any good playwright writes about characters in stressful situations who are often in a state of conflict not only with the world around them and the people in that world, but also within themselves. And you probably know from personal experience that when these conflicts occur people do not necessarily utter the most perfect of grammatical/poetic/ syntactic statements, phrases, or sentences. Joy and delight, pain and sorrow often come sweeping through in the way things are said, in the incoherence of the phrases, the running together of normally disassoci- ated ideas, and even in the sounds of the words themselves.

The tremendous advantage of the period in which Shakespeare was set- ting his plays down on paper and how they first appeared in print was that when characters were rational and in control of self and situation, their phrasing and sentences (and poetic structure) would appear to be quite normal even to a modern eye - but when things were go- ing wrong, so sentences and phrasing (and poetic structure) would become highly erratic. But the Quince type eccentricities are rarely allowed to stand. Sadly, in tidying , most modern texts usually make the text far too clean, thus setting rationality when none originally existed.

THE SECOND ESSENTIAL DIFFERENCE BETWEEN THE TWO TEXTS
SPEAKING, ARGUING, DEBATING

Having discovered what and how you/your character is thinking is only the first stage of the work - you/it then have to speak aloud, in a society that absolutely loved to speak - and not only speak ideas (con- tent) but to speak entertainingly so as to keep listeners enthralled (and this was especially so when you have little content to offer and have to mask it somehow - think of today 's television adverts and political spin doctors as a parallel and you get the picture). Indeed one of the Elizabethan 'how to win an argument' books was very precise about this - George Puttenham, *The Art of English Poesie* (1589).

A: ELIZABETHAN SCHOOLING

All educated classes could debate/argue at the drop of a hat, for both boys (in 'petty-schools') and girls (by books and tutors) were trained in what was known overall as the art of rhetoric, which itself was split into three parts

- first, how to distinguish the real from false appearances/outward show (think of the three caskets in *The Merchant of Venice* where the language on the gold and silver caskets enticingly, and deceptively, seems to offer hopes of great personal rewards that are dashed when the language is carefully explored, whereas once the apparent threat on the lead casket is carefully analysed the reward therein is the greatest that could be hoped for)
- second, how to frame your argument on one of 'three great grounds'; honour/morality; justice/legality; and, when all else fails, expedience/practicality.
- third, how to order and phrase your argument so winsomely that your audience will vote for you no matter how good the opposition - and there were well over two hundred rules and variations by which winning could be achieved, all of which had to be assimilated before a child's education was considered over and done with.

B: THINKING ON YOUR FEET: I.E. THE QUICK, DEFT , RAPID MODIFICATION OF EACH TINY THOUGHT

The Elizabethan/therefore your character/therefore you were also trained to explore and modify your thoughts as you spoke - never would you see a sentence in its entirety and have it perfectly worked out in your mind before you spoke (unless it was a deliberately written, formal public declaration, as with the Officer of the Court in The Winter' s Tale, reading the charges against Hermione). Thus after uttering your very first phrase, you might expand it, or modify it, deny it, change it, and so on throughout the whole sentence and speech.

From the poet Samuel Coleridge Taylor there is a wonderful description of how Shakespeare puts thoughts together like "a serpent twisting and untwisting in its own strength," that is, with one thought springing out of the one previous. Treat each new phrase as a fresh unravelling of the serpent's coil. What is discovered (and therefore said) is only revealed as the old coil/phrase disappears revealing a new coil in its place. The new coil is the new thought. The old coil moves/disappears because the previous phrase is finished with as soon as it is spoken.

C: MODERN APPLICATION

It is very rarely we speak dispassionately in our 'real' lives, after all thoughts give rise to feelings, feelings give rise to thoughts, and we usually speak both together - unless

1/ we're trying very hard for some reason to control ourselves and not give ourselves away

2/ or the volcano of emotions within us is so strong that we cannot control ourselves, and feelings swamp thoughts

3/ and sometimes whether deliberately or unconsciously we colour words according to our feelings; the humanity behind the words so revealed is instantly understandable.

D: HOW THE ORIGINAL TEXTS NATURALLY ENHANCE/ UNDERSCORE THIS CONTROL OR RELEASE

The amazing thing about the way all Elizabethan/early Jacobean texts were first set down (the term used to describe the printed words on the page being 'orthography'), is that it was flexible, it allowed for such variations to be automatically set down without fear of grammatical repercussion.

So if Shakespeare heard Juliet's nurse working hard to try to convince Juliet that the Prince's nephew Juliet is being forced to (bigamously) marry, instead of setting the everyday normal

'O he's a lovely gentleman'

which the modern texts HAVE to set, the first printings were permitted to set

'O hee's a Lovely Gentleman'

suggesting that something might be going on inside the Nurse that causes her to release such excessive extra energy.

E: BE CAREFUL

This needs to be stressed very carefully: the orthography doesn't dictate to you/force you to accept exactly what it means. The orthography simply suggests you might want to explore this moment further or more deeply.

In other words, simply because of the flexibility with which the Elizabethans/Shakespeare could set down on paper what they heard in their minds or wanted their listeners to hear, in addition to all the modern acting necessities of character - situation, objective, intention, action, and tactics the original Shakespeare texts offer pointers to where feelings (either emotional or intellectual, or when combined together as passion, both) are also evident.

SUMMARY

BASIC APPROACH TO THE SPEECHES SHOWN BELOW

(after reading the 'background')

1/ first use the modem version shown in the first column: by doing so you can discover
- the basic plot line of what's happening to the character, and
- the first set of conflicts/obstacles impinging on the character as a result of the situation or actions of other characters
- the supposed grammatical and poetical correctnesses of the speech

2/ then you can explore
- any acting techniques you'd apply to any modem soliloquy, including establishing for the character
- the given circumstances of the scene
- their outward state of being (who they are sociologically, etc.)
- their intentions and objectives
- the resultant action and tactics they decide to pursue

3/ when this is complete, turn to the First Folio version of the text, shown on the facing page: this will help you discover and explore
- the precise thinking and debating process so essential to an understanding of any Shakespeare text
- the moments when the text is NOT grammatically or poetically as correct as the modern texts would have you believe, which will in tum help you recognise
- the moments of conflict and struggle stemming from within the character itself
- the sense of fun and enjoyment the Shakespeare language nearly always offers you no matter how dire the situation

4/ should you wish to further explore even more the differences between the two texts, the commentary that follows discusses how the First Folio has been changed, and what those alterations might mean for the human arc of the speech

NOTES ON HOW THESE SPEECHES ARE SET UP

For each of the speeches the first page will include the Background on the speech and other information including number of lines, approximate timing and who is addressed. Then will follow a spread which shows the modern text version on the left and the First Folio version on the right, followed by a page of Commentary.

PROBABLE TIMING: (shown on the Background page before the speeches begin, set below the number of lines) 0.45 = a forty-five second speech

SYMBOLS & ABBREVIATIONS IN THE COMMENTARY AND TEXT

F: the First Folio

mt.: modern texts

F # followed by a number: the number of the sentence under discussion in the First Folio version of the speech, thus F #7 would refer to the seventh sentence

mt. # followed by a numb er: the number of the sentence under discussion in the modern text version of the speech, thus mt. #5 would refer to the fifth sentence

/#, (e.g. 3/7): the first number refers to the number of capital letters in the passage under discussion; the second refers to the number of long spellings therein

within a quotation from the speech: / indicates where one verse line ends and a fresh one starts

[ ] : set around words in both texts when Fl sets one word , mt another

{ } : some minor alteration has been made, in a speech built up, where, a word or phrase will be changed, added, or removed

{†} : this symbol shows where a sizeable part of the text is omitted

TERMS FOUND IN THE COMMENTARY
OVERALL

1/ **orthography**: the capitalization, spellings, punctuation of the First Folio
SIGNS OF IMPORTANT DISCOVERIES/ARGUMENTS WITHIN A FIRST FOLIO SPEECH

2/ **major punctuation**: colons and semicolons: since the Shakespeare texts are based so much on the art of debate and argument, the importance of F1 's major punctuation must not be underestimated, for both the semi-colon (;) and colon (:) mark a moment of importance for the character, either for itself, as a moment of discovery or revelation, or as a key point in a discussion, argument or debate that it wishes to impress upon other characters onstage

as a rule of thumb:

a/ the more frequent colon (:) suggests that whatever the power of the point discovered or argued, the character is not side-tracked and can con-tinue with the argument - as such, the colon can be regarded as a **logical** connection

b/ the far less frequent semicolon (;) suggests that because of the power inherent in the point discovered or argued, the character is side-tracked and momentarily loses the argument and falls back into itself or can only continue the argument with great difficulty - as such, the semicolon should be regarded as an **emotional** connection

3/ **surround phrases**: phrase(s) surrounded by major punctuation, or a combination of major punctuation and the end or beginning of a sentence: thus these phrases seem to be of especial importance for both character and speech, well worth exploring as key to the argument made and /or emotions released

DIALOGUE NOT FOUND IN THE FIRST FOLIO
∞ set where modern texts add dialogue from a quarto text which has not been included in Fl

A LOOSE RULE OF THUMB TO THE THINKING PROCESS OF A FIRST FOLIO CHARACTER

1/ mental discipline/**intellect**: a section where capitals dominate suggests that the intellectual reason ing behind what is being spoken or discovered is of more concern than the personal response beneath it

2/ feelings/**emotions**: a section where long spellings dominate suggests that the personal response to what is being spoken or discovered is of more concern than the intellectual reasoning behind it

3/ **passion**: a section where both long spellings and capitals are present in almost equal proportions suggests that both mind and emotion/feelings are inseparable, and thus the character is speaking passionately

SIGNS OF LESS THAN GRAMMATICAL THINKING WITHIN A FIRST FOLIO SPEECH

1/ **onrush**: sometimes thoughts are coming so fast that several topics are joined together as one long sentence suggesting that the F character's mind is working very quickly, or that his/her emotional state is causing some concern: most mod ern texts split such a sentence into several grammatically correct parts (the opening speech of *As You Like It* is a fine example, where F's long 18 line opening sentence is split into six): while the modern texts' resetting may be syntactically correct, the F moment is nowhere near as calm as the revisions suggest

2/ **fast-link**: sometimes F shows thoughts moving so quickly for a character that the connecting punctuation between disparate topics is merely a comma, suggesting that there is virtually no pause in springing from one idea to the next: unfortunately most modern texts rarely allow this to stand, instead replacing the obviously disturbed comma with a grammatical period, once more creating calm that it seems the original texts never intended to show

FIRST FOLIO SIGNS OF WHEN VERBAL GAME PLAYING HAS TO STOP

1/ **non-embellished:** a section with neither capitals nor long spellings suggests that what is being discovered or spoken is so important to the character that there is no time to guss it up with vocal or mental excesses: an unusual moment of self-control

2/ **short sentence:** coming out of a society where debate was second nature, man y of Shakespeare's characters speak in long sentences in which ideas are stated, explored, redefined and summarized all before moving onto the next idea in the argument, discovery or debate: the longer sentence is the sign of a rhetorically trained mind used to public speaking (oratory), but at times an idea or discovery is so startling or inevitable that length is either unnecessary or impossible to maintain : hence the occasional very important short sentence suggests that there is no time for the niceties of oratorical adornment with which to sugar the pill - verbal games are at an end and now the basic core of the issue must be faced

3/ **monosyllabic:** with English being composed of two strands, the polysyllabic (stemming from French, Italian, Latin and Greek), and the monosyllabic (from the Anglo-Saxon), each strand has two distinct functions: the polysyllabic words are often used when there is time for fanciful elaboration and rich description (which could be described as 'excessive rhetoric') while the monosyllabic occur when, literally, there is no other way of putting a basic question or comment - Juliet's "Do you love me? I know thou wilt say aye" is a classic example of both monosyllables and non-embellishment: with monosyllables, only the naked truth is being spoken, nothing is hidden

Monologues from Shakespeare's First Folio for Women: *The Histories*

The First Part of Henry the Sixt

Joan La Pucelle / Joanne Puzel

Dolphin, I am by birth a Shepheards Daughter,
between 1.2.72–92

Background: this is the less than flattering English version of the French savior, the woman later known as St. Joan. Having laid claims to 'a Vision sent to her from Heaven/...to rayse this tedious siege/And drive the English forth the bounds of France' and to possess 'The spirit of deepe Prophecie', and having seen through the attempt of the French nobles to test her 'deepe Prophecie' by substituting Reigneir for Charles, the following is her first major speech in the play, explaining who she is and why she has dared to come and see the King.

Style: one on one in front of a small group

Where: the French court, just after their defeat at Orleance

To Whom: Charles the Dolphin, in front of Alanson and the Bastard of Orleance

# of Lines: 21

Probable Timing: 1.00 minutes

Take note: The original suggests a young woman not as relaxed as her modern counterpart—a country girl socially out of her depth but determined to make her point.

Joan La Pucelle

1   Dolphin, I am by birth a shepherd's daughter,
    My wit untrain'd in any kind of art .

2   Heaven and our Lady gracious hath it pleas'd
    To shine on my contemptible estate .

3   Lo , [whilst] I waited on my tender lambs ,
    And to sun's parching heat display'd my cheeks ,
    God's Mother deigned to appear to me,
    And in a vision full of majesty
    Will'd me to leave my base vocation
    And free my country from calamity .

4   Her aid she promis'd, and assur'd success ;
    In complete glory she reveal'd her self :
    And whereas I was black and swart before,
    With those clear rays , which she infus'd on me
    That beauty am I blest with, which you may see .

5   Ask me what question thou canst possible,
    And I will answer unpremeditated ;
    My courage try by combat, if thou dar'st,
    And thou shalt find that I exceed my sex .

6   Resolve on this : thou shalt be fortunate
    If thou receive me for thy warlike mate .

Puzel

1 Dolphin, I am by birth a Shepheards Daughter,
My wit untrayn'd in any kind of Art :
Heaven and our Lady gracious hath it pleas'd
To shine on my contemptible estate .

2 Loe, [whilest] I wayted on my tender Lambes,
And to Sunnes parching heat display'd my cheekes,
Gods Mother deigned to appeare to me,
And in a Vision full of Majestie,
Will'd me to leave my base Vocation,
And free my Countrey from Calamitie :
Her ayde she promis'd, and assur'd successe .

3 In compleat Glory shee reveal'd her selfe :
And whereas I was black and swart before,
With those cleare Rayes, which shee infus'd on me,
That beautie am I blest with, which you may see .

4 Aske me what question thou canst possible,
And I will answer unpremeditated :
My Courage trie by Combat, if thou dar'st,
And thou shalt finde that I exceed my Sex .

5 Resolve on this, thou shalt be fortunate,
If thou receive me for thy Warlike Mate .

- the F opening sentence, twice as long as its modern equivalent, suggests a blurt rather than the modern rewrite which presents more control

- the fact that 'Her ayde she promis'd, and assur'd successe' ends F's sentence #2 rather than starting the modern #4 suggests a stronger oratorical persuasive need rather than a grammatical correctness

- the F extra breath thoughts omitted by the modern texts again suggest a strong need to persuade, especially in the rushed last sentence

- each of the four F colons either sums up what has been said or leads to an important conclusion in what follows

- the importance to her of 'Gods Mother' is revealed not only in the capitalization, but also in that she is referred to most unusually as 'shee' twice in sentence #3, which is further emphasized by the phrase 'In compleat Glory shee reveal'd her selfe' starting F #3 instead of being the second line of modern text #4

- there are rapid swings between capitals dominating the text (the opening of sentence #1; lines 2-6 of sentence #2; the last four lines of the speech) and longer spellings (the opening of sentence #2 and the first three lines of sentence #3)—suggesting that the struggle to maintain intellectual clarity is often swamped with Pucell's personal feelings breaking through

The First Part of Henry the Sixt
Countess/Countesse

Is this the Scourge of France ?
between 2.3.15–42

Background: the French Countesse of 'Overgne' has invited English Talbot as a guest to her home, intending to break all the known rules of chivalry and take him prisoner. Confident that her plan has worked, she now insults him to his face—unaware that Talbot has brought his forces with him, and that she will become his captive instead.

Style: as part of a possible three-handed scene

Where: in the home of the Countesse

To Whom: Talbot, perhaps in front of the Porter, as well as other guests—though none such are indicated in the stage directions

# of Lines: 20

Probable Timing: 0.50 minutes

Take Note: Though the difference in sentence structure between the two texts is minimal, once again the orthographical variations of F show the mood swings the Countesse goes through as she thinks Talbot is her prisoner.

Countess

1   Is this the scourge of France ?

2   Is this the Talbot, so much fear'd abroad
    That with his name the mothers still their babes ?

3   I see report is fabulous and false .

4   I thought I should have seen some Hercules,
    A second Hector, for his grim aspect
    And large proportion of his strong knit limbs .

5   Alas, this is a child, a silly dwarf !

6   It cannot be this weak and writhled shrimp
    Should strike such terror to his enemies .

---

7   If thou be he, then art thou prisoner { }

    To me, blood-thirsty lord ;
    And for that cause I train'd thee to my house .

8   Long time thy shadow hath been thrall to me,
    For in my gallery thy picture hangs ;
    But now the substance shall endure the like,
    And I will chain these legs and arms of thine,
    That hast by tyranny these many years
    Wasted our country , slain our citizens,
    And sent our sons and husbands captive .

Countesse

1   Is this the Scourge of France ?

2   Is this the Talbot, so much fear'd abroad ?
    That with his Name the Mothers still their Babes ?

3   I see Report is fabulous and false .

4   I thought I should have seene some Hercules,
    A second Hector, for his grim aspect,
    And large proportion of his strong knit Limbes .

5   Alas, this is a Child, a silly Dwarfe :
    It cannot be, this weake and writhled shrimpe
    Should strike such terror to his Enemies .

---

6   If thou be he, then art thou Prisoner { }

    To me, blood-thirstie Lord :
    And for that cause I trayn'd thee to my House .

7   Long time thy shadow hath been thrall to me,
    For in my Gallery thy Picture hangs :
    But now the substance shall endure the like,
    And I will chayne these Legges and Armes of thine,
    That hast by Tyrannie these many yeeres
    Wasted our Countrey, slaine our Citizens,
    And sent our Sonnes and Husbands captivate .

- the one sentence difference (F #5 split in two, mt. #5-#6) allows the F Countesse to sustain her scorn for a slightly lengthier and thus more continuous attack, which is also helped by the extra thought set in F splitting the line 'It cannot be, this weake and…' into two insults rather than one

- the speech essentially falls into four parts, perhaps suggesting control of public rhetoric at times and a more personal agenda coming through at others

  a. the first three triumphant F sentences are governed by a purely intellectual release (7/0)

  b. then, as the personal insults towards Talbot are let loose (F #4-#5), her own feelings come flooding through and the put downs become much more passionate (6 more capitals joined by the first five long-spelled words of the speech)

  c. and then, as the Countesse announces that Talbot has been captured by her (F #6 and the first two lines of #7), an (almost) purely intellectual statement is regained (5/1)

  d. finally, in the last five lines of the speech, as she describes what she will do to him and why, so her passions break through even greater than before (7/7)

The First Part of Henry the Sixt

Joan La Pucelle/Pucell

First let me tell you whom you have condemn'd
5.4.36–53 & 86–91

Background: Pucell has been captured by the English. Neither their attempts to discredit her by producing her supposed father, nor her attempts to escape death by claiming she is pregnant have succeeded. She has been condemned to die, burnt at the stake, and the following is her response. One note: in the action of the play, the pregnancy plea comes before the second part (the last two sentences) of the speech as shown below.

Style: either a three-handed scene, or a plea to a small group in front of a larger one

Where: the camp of the English Duke of Yorke

To Whom: Yorke, Warwicke, and perhaps Yorke's forces

# of Lines: 29

Probable Timing: 1.30 minutes

Take Note: There is a tremendous grandstanding, barnstorming quality to the F speech. This doesn't necessarily mean that it is an artificially grand speech, spoken by an exquisite and practiced debater. Given the circumstances (a farm girl fighting for her life), it simply suggests that she is arguing as passionately as she knows how, warts and all. The modern sentence restructuring and inability to reproduce the F orthographical variations present a much more straightforward speech than was originally set.

La Pucelle

1   First let me tell you whom you have condemn'd :
     Not [one] begotten of a shepherd swain ,
     But issued from the progeny of kings ;
     [Virtuous] and holy, chosen from above,
     By inspiration of celestial grace,
     To work exceeding miracles on earth .

2   I never had to do with wicked spirits .

3   But you, that are polluted with your lusts ,
     Stain'd with the guiltless blood of innocents,
     Corrupt and tainted with a thousand vices,
     Because you want the grace that others have,
     You judge it straight a thing impossible
     To compass wonders but by help of devils .

4   No, misconceived !

5   [Joan of Arc] hath been
     A virgin from her tender infancy ,
     Chaste, and immaculate in very thought,
     Whose maiden-blood, thus rigorously effus'd,
     Will cry for vengeance at the gates of heaven .

---

6   Then lead me hence ; with whom I leave my curse :
     May never glorious sun reflex his beams
     Upon the country where you make abode :
     But darkness and the gloomy shade of death
     Environ you, till mischief and despair ,
     Drive you to break your necks or hang yourselves !

Pucell

1 First let me tell you whom you have condemn'd ;
  Not [me], begotten of a Shepheard Swaine,
  But issued from the Progeny of Kings .

2 [Vertuous] and Holy, chosen from above,
  By inspiration of Celestiall Grace,
  To worke exceeding myracles on earth .

3 I never had to do with wicked Spirits .

4 But you that are polluted with your lustes,
  Stain'd with the guiltlesse blood of Innocents,
  Corrupt and tainted with a thousand Vices :
  Because you want the grace that others have,
  You judge it straight a thing impossible
  To compasse Wonders, but by helpe of divels .

5 No misconceyved, [Jone of Aire] hath beene
  A Virgin from her tender infancie,
  Chaste, and immaculate in very thought,
  Whose Maiden-blood thus rigorously effus'd,
  Will cry for Vengeance, at the Gates of Heaven .

6 Then lead me hence : with whom I leave my curse .

7 May never glorious Sunne reflex his beames
  Upon the Countrey where you make abode :
  But darknesse, and the gloomy shade of death
  Inviron you, till Mischeefe and Dispaire,
  Drive you to break your necks, or hang your selves .

- until the very last sentence, most of her capitals deal with almost biblical concepts—'Holy', 'Celestiall', 'Grace'—and almost naively romantic absolute concepts—'Progeny of Kings', 'Virgin', 'Maiden-blood', 'Shepheard Swaine'—while many of the released words (long spellings) deal with the struggle between the uglier sides of life—'lustes' and 'misconceyved' versus 'myracles' and 'guiltlesse'

- that she is working very hard and is very moved at the start of the speech can be seen in

  a. the (emotional) semicolon ending the first line

  b. the fact that whereas modern texts set F #1-#2 as one long sentence, the totally ungrammatical F sentence #2 suggests a greater and not necessarily logical need to stress the holiness of her origins and acts

  c. the six opening F lines (F #1-#2) show no consistency, but keep switching from (enforced?) calm (line 1); to a passionate statement (line 2); to an intellectual statement (lines 3-5); and eventually to an emotional release (line 6)

- then things calm somewhat until the end of F sentence #4 and the start of F #5 when another concentrated passionate flourish is released (3/5 in just two lines), and this pattern of a line or two of relative calm followed by two or three lines of release is maintained till the end of the speech

- the rhythm of the F speech is occasionally very different from its modern counterpart, with five extra thoughts that spell out tiny extra details she feels are needed to strengthen her case, and with three moments where modern texts have added extra punctuation each of which slows down the passion of her flow

The Second Part of Henry the Sixt

Eleanor/Elianor

Why droopes my Lord like over_ripen'd Corn,
1.2.1–16

Background: Margaret's complaint about Elianor's airs and graces (the following two speeches) has some justification, since Gloster's wife entertains ambitions way beyond being merely the wife of the Protector of the Realm, even dreaming of becoming Queen herself. In this, Elianor's first speech of the play, her naked ambition goes so far as to counsel her husband Gloster to consider deposing his nephew Henry.

Style: as part of a two-handed scene

Where: the Glosters' private chambers

To Whom: her husband Gloster

# of Lines: 16

Probable Timing: 0.50 minutes

Take Note: While the sentence structure of the two texts parallel one another, F's orthography offers a fascinating glimpse into the care with which Elianor finally urges her husband Gloster to treasonous thoughts.

Eleanor

1 Why droops my lord, like over-ripen'd corn
   Hanging the head at Ceres' plenteous load ?

2 Why doth the great Duke [Humphrey] knit his brows ,
   As frowning at the favors of the world ?

3 Why are thine eyes fix'd to the sullen earth,
   Gazing on that which seems to dim thy sight ?

4 What seest thou there ?

5   King Henry's diadem,
   Enchas'd with all the honors of the world ?

6 If so, gaze on, and grovel on thy face,
   Until thy head be circled with the same .

7 Put forth thy hand, reach at the glorious gold .

8 What, is't too short ?

9   I'll lengthen it with mine,
   And having both together heav'd it up,
   We'll both together lift our heads to heaven,
   And never more abase our sight so low
   As to vouchsafe one glance unto the ground .

Elianor

1   Why droopes my Lord like over_ripen'd Corn,
    Hanging the head at Ceres plenteous load ?

2   Why doth the Great Duke [Humfrey] knit his browes,
    As frowning at the Favours of the world ?

3   Why are thine eyes fixt to the sullen earth,
    Gazing on that which seemes to dimme thy sight ?

4   What seest thou there ?

5   King Henries Diadem,
    Inchac'd with all the Honors of the world ?

6   If so, Gaze on, and grovell on thy face,
    Untill thy head be circled with the same .

7   Put forth thy hand, reach at the glorious Gold .

8   What, is't too short ?

9   Ile lengthen it with mine,
    And having both together heav'd it up,
    Wee'l both together lift our heads to heaven,
    And never more abase our sight so low,
    As to vouchsafe one glance unto the ground.

- as Elianor openly states that there is no need for him to be bowed down with the cares of others, her first two sentences suggest she is in full mental control of her actions (7/3 in just four lines)

- then, as she all but accuses Gloster of being willfully blind to the advantages facing him (F #3), so emotions momentarily take over (0/2)

- but as she openly brings forth the subject of the throne and all the riches thereunto (F #5-6), her mental control returns and passion starts to break through (5/3)

- and then, as she urges Gloster to join her in taking the crown for themselves, so embellishments are almost completely leached out (1/1 in six lines, four of which have no embellishments at all)—as if even contemplation of the act has to be very carefully voiced

- it's also fascinating that, despite her mind working quite hard throughout (13/9 in sixteen lines) logic may not be her strong suit, since there is no major punctuation anywhere in the speech

The Second Part of Henry the Sixt
Queen/Queene
My Lord of Suffolke, say, is this the guise ?
1.3.42–64

Background: having treated legal petitioners extremely brusquely, Margaret speaks her dissatisfaction both about her marriage and her husband Henry; about her personal lack of power thanks to Gloster, uncle and close advisor to the King; and about the governance of the country.

Style: as part of a two-handed scene

Where: unspecified, a public space in or near the palace that the petitoners have just left

To Whom: Suffolke

# of Lines: 23

Probable Timing: 1.10 minutes

Take Note: F's orthography underlines the amazing debating and analytical quality of Margaret's mind and her ability to express herself freely with great feeling.

Queen

1   My Lord of Suffolk , say, is this the guise,
    Is this the fashions in the court of England ?

2   Is this the government of [Britain's] isle ,
    And this the royalty of Albion's king ?

3   What, shall King Henry be a pupil still
    Under the surly [Gloucester's] governance ?

4   Am I a queen in title and in style ,
    And must be made a subject to a duke ?

5   I tell thee, [Pole], when in the city Tours
    Thou ran'st a-tilt in honor of my love
    And stol'st away the ladies' hearts of France ;
    I thought King Henry had resembled thee
    In courage, courtship, and proportion ;
    But all his mind is bent to holiness ,
    To number Ave-Maries on his beads ;
    His champions are the prophets and apostles,
    His weapons, holy saws of sacred writ,
    His study is his tilt-yard, and his loves
    Are brazen images of canonized saints .

6   I would the college of the Cardinals
    Would choose him Pope and carry him to Rome,
    And set the triple crown upon his head—
    That were a state fit for his holiness .

Queene

1   My Lord of Suffolke, say, is this the guise ?

2   Is this the Fashions in the Court of England ?

3   Is this the Government of [Britaines] Ile ?

4   And this the Royaltie of Albions King ?

5   What, shall King Henry be a Pupill still,
Under the surly [Glosters] Governance ?

6   Am I a Queene in Title and in Stile,
And must be made a Subject to a Duke ?

7   I tell thee [Poole], when in the Citie Tours
Thou ran'st a_tilt in honor of my Love,
And stol'st away the Ladies hearts of France ;
I thought King Henry had resembled thee,
In Courage, Courtship, and Proportion :
But all his minde is bent to Holinesse,
To number Ave-Maries on his Beades :
His Champions, are the Prophets and Apostles,
His Weapons, holy Sawes of sacred Writ,
His Studie is his Tilt-yard, and his Loves
Are brazen Images of Canonized Saints .

8   I would the Colledge of the Cardinalls
Would chuse him Pope, and carry him to Rome,
And set the Triple Crowne upon his Head ;
That were a State fit for his Holinesse .

- F's orthography underlines the amazing debating and analytical quality of Margaret's mind and her ability to express herself freely with great feeling.

- F's opening relentless attack of four separate questions set as four separate short sentences presents much more demand than the modern reduction of the event (by resetting F #1-2 and #3-4 as just two sentences)

- the amazing number of capitalized words (56 in twenty-three lines) gives testament to the brilliance of her mind

- and of the 11 longer-spellings, six are to be found in three clusters all dismissive of her new husband, viz.

  > "But all his minde is bent to Holinesse,/To number Ave-Maries on his Beades :"

  > "I would the Colledge of the Cardinalls"

  > "And set the Triple Crowne upon his Head ; / That were a State fit for his Holinesse ."

- and what are almost surround phrases go straight to the heart of her problem.

  > "; I thought King Henry had resembled thee,/In Courage, Courtship, and Proportion :/But all his minde is bent to Holinesse,/To number Ave-Maries on his Beades :"

  and

  > "; That were a State fit for his Holinesse . "

- the two (emotional) semi-colons focus on her desire for Henry to either be like Suffolke, or to be chosen as Pope and so be out of her hair

- there are just four extra thoughts but each highlights her key concerns—one (F #5) focuses on her enemy Gloster; the first two in F #7 heap extra praise on Suffolke; and the last in F #7 is highly contemptuous of Henry's religious fervor

The Second Part of Henry the Sixt
Queen/Queene

Not all these Lords do vex me halfe so much
1.3.75-87

Background: Margaret definitively expresses her loathing for Elianor, Gloster's wife, who continually insults her about her father's lack of territories (the English assessment of her father Reigneir is to dismiss him as 'no better than an Earle,/Although in glorious Titles he excell').

Style: as part of a two-handed scene

Where: unspecified, a public space in or near the palace

To Whom: Suffolke

# of Lines: 13

Probable Timing: 0.45 minutes

Take Note: The depth of Margaret's hatred for Elianor is even more marked in both F's sentence structure (just two sentences as opposed to most modern texts' much weaker four) and, especially, orthography.

Queen

1   Not all these lords do vex me half so much
     As that proud dame, the Lord Protector's wife :
     She sweeps it through the court with troops of ladies,
     More like an empress then Duke Humphrey's wife,
     Strangers in court do take her for the Queen .

2   She bears a duke's revenues on her back ,
     And in her heart she scornes our poverty .

3   Shall I not live to be aveng'd on her ?

4   Contemptuous base-born callot as she is,
     She vaunted 'mongst her minions t'other day,
     The very train of her worst wearing gown
     Was better worth then all my father's lands,
     Till Suffolk gave two dukedoms for his daughter .

Queene

1   Not all these Lords do vex me halfe so much,
As that prowd Dame, the Lord Protectors Wife :
She sweepes it through the Court with troups of Ladies,
More like an Empresse, then Duke Humphreyes Wife :
Strangers in Court, doe take her for the Queene :
She beares a Dukes Revenewes on her backe,
And in her heart she scornes our Povertie :
Shall I not live to be aveng'd on her ?

2   Contemptuous base-borne Callot as she is,
She vaunted 'mongst her Minions t'other day,
The very trayne of her worst wearing Gowne,
Was better worth then all my Fathers Lands,
Till Suffolke gave two Dukedomes for his Daughter .

- the speech is astoundingly intellectually passionate (24/16 in 13 lines): the first ferocious sentence is driven logically as well as passionately (for there are four colons plus the 16 capitals and 11 long spellings in just eight lines), while the second sentence initially eases off somewhat (2/1 in the first two lines) then explodes once more (6/4) in the final insulting recollection

- the surround phrases ' : Strangers in Court, doe take her for the Queene : ' and ' : Shall I not live to be aveng'd on her ? ' immediately throw into focus from where her hatred and intention stem

- if the second surround phrase just listed were overheard by Elianor, she would have every reason to fear for her future—for it is the only ice-cold unembellished line in the speech

The Second Part of Henry the Sixt
Queen/Queene

Oh, let me intreat thee cease, give me thy hand,
3.2.339–356

Background: This is Margaret's attempt to deal with Suffolke's cursing anger (following his banishment) by reasoning with him.

Style: as part of a two-handed scene

Where: the English court in London

To Whom: her lover, Suffolke

# of Lines: 19

Probable Timing: 1.00 minutes

Take Note: The emotional content of scene and speech is obvious in both texts. What F's orthography offers are additional glimpses into the small and continuous cracks in Margaret's emotional make-up that can only be guessed at in the modern texts.

Queen

1   O , let me entreat thee cease .

2   Give me thy hand,
That I may dew it with my mournful tears ;
Nor let the rain of heaven wet this place
To wash away my woeful monuments .

3   O , could this kiss be printed in thy hand,
That thou mightst think upon these by the seal ,
Through whom a thousand sighs are breath'd for thee !

4   So get thee gone, that I may know my grief ,
'Tis but surmis'd whiles thou art standing by,
As one that surfeits thinking on a want .

5   I will repeal thee, or, be well assur'd,
Adventure to be banished myself ;
And banished I am, if but from thee .

6   Go, speak not to me ; even now be gone .

7   O , go not yet .

8   Even thus two friends condemn'd
Embrace, and kiss , and take ten thousand leaves,
Loather a hundred times to part then die .

9   Yet now farewell, and farewell life with thee !

Queene

1 Oh, let me intreat thee cease, give me thy hand,
   That I may dew it with my mournfull teares :
   Nor let the raine of heaven wet this place,
   To wash away my wofull Monuments .

2 Oh, could this kisse be printed in thy hand,
   That thou might'st thinke upon these by the Seale,
   Through whom a thousand sighes are breath'd for thee .

3 So get thee gone, that I may know my greefe,
   'Tis but surmiz'd, whiles thou art standing by,
   As one that surfets, thinking on a want :
   I will repeale thee, or be well assur'd,
   Adventure to be banished my selfe :
   And banished I am, if but from thee .

4 Go, speake not to me ; even now be gone .

5 Oh go not yet .

6   Even thus, two Friends condemn'd,
   Embrace, and kisse, and take ten thousand leaves,
   Loather a hundred times to part then dye ;
   Yet now farewell, and farewell Life with thee .

- the fact that three F sentences (#1, #3, and #6) are set as onrushes, rather than each being split in two by most modern texts, suggests somewhat less control than modern texts would care to suppose – especially in F #1, where what modern texts set as their sentence #2 was originally shown as a fast-link connecting blurt by F

- though the number of emotional long spellings far outweighs capitals (4/19), they all support her words and argument rather than distract from them

- that whatever control Margaret may be able to muster begins to weaken towards the end of the speech is shown by the two unusually short F sentences #4-5, followed by the only two (emotional) semi-colons of the speech, the first linking the two appallingly hurtful (for both) commands

    " Go, speake not to me ; even now be gone."

and the second preceding the irrevocable

    " ; Yet now farewell, and farewell Life with thee."

the latter containing one of the only 4 capitals in the eighteen line speech

- though there are only four extra breath thoughts in F #1, #3, and #6, each are testament to her longing for him

- in comparison to her earlier attempts to bamboozle Henry, this speech's imagery shows far greater dignity

The Third Part of Henry the Sixt
{Queene} Margaret

King Lewis, and Lady Bona, heare me speake,
3.3.65–77

Background: in the see-saw battle for the English Crown currently
the Yorkists are victorious. King Henry has escaped to Scotland,
and Queen Margaret and their son have arrived in Paris to seek
sanctuary and aid from Lewis, King of France, to overthrow the
newly crowned Yorkist Edward. In the midst of her appeal to
an already dubious King arrives the Yorkist Warwicke, offering
to Lewis on behalf of 'Edward, King of Albion' friendship, via a
'League of Amitie', the 'Amitie' to be sealed by marriage between
Edward and the French King's sister, the Lady Bona. The following
is Margaret's attempt to block the proposal.

Style: address mainly to two people in front of a larger group

Where: the French Court

To Whom: the King of France and his sister Lady Bona, in front of
his Admiral, Margaret's son, her supporter Oxford, and the Yorkist
Warwicke

# of Lines: 13

Probable Timing: 0.45 minutes

Take Note: Though both sentence structures match, F's orthography
provides a wonderful map as to how Margaret makes her anti-Ed-
ward argument

Margaret

1   King Lewis, and Lady Bona, hear me speak
     Before you answer Warwick .

2   His demand
     Springs not from Edward's well-meant honest love,
     But from deceit, bred by necessity ;
     For how can tyrants safely govern home,
     Unless abroad they purchase great alliance ?

3   To prove him tyrant this reason may suffice,
     That Henry liveth still ; but were he dead,
     Yet here Prince Edward stands, King Henry's son .

4   Look therefore, Lewis, that by this league and

                                           marriage
     Thou draw not on thy danger, and dis°honor ;
     For though usurpers sway the rule a while,
     Yet heav'ns are just, and time suppresseth wrongs .

Margaret

1   King Lewis, and Lady Bona, heare me speake,
Before you answer Warwicke .

2   His demand
Springs not from Edwards well-meant honest Love,
But from Deceit, bred by Necessitie :
For how can Tyrants safely governe home,
Unlesse abroad they purchase great allyance?

3   To prove him Tyrant, this reason may suffice,
That Henry liveth still : but were hee dead,
Yet here Prince Edward stands, King Henries Sonne .

4   Looke therefore Lewis, that by this League and Mariage
Thou draw not on thy Danger, and Dis-honor :
For though Usurpers sway the rule a while,
Yet Heav'ns are just, and Time suppresseth Wrongs .

- F #1 opens with passion (5/3), the extra comma ending the first line stressing the great care she is taking to try and save the situation

- the first two and a half lines of F #2, her denial of all that Warwicke stands for, is purely intellectual (4/0), but in the final two lines of the sentence denouncing Edward, her emotions break through (1/3)

- as she is prepared to offer proof of Edward's tyranny, her intellect again comes to the fore (2/0 in the opening one and a half lines of F #3), the extra breath thought once more testifying to the care she is taking

- and then, as she warns against the 'Danger, and Dishonor' if Lewis were to side with Yorkist Edward, her intellect is given full sway (an amazing 13/3 in the final five and a half lines of the speech)

The Third Part of Henry the Sixt
{Queene Elizabeth} Gray

Why Brother Rivers, are you yet to learne
between 4.4.2–35

Background: Yorkist Edward has married an impoverished English widow, Lady Gray, thus breaking off marriage overtures made on his behalf by Warwicke to Lady Bona, sister to the King of France. The marriage has given a doubly huge boost to the Lancastrian opposition. First, the King of France, as a result of the perceived insult to his sister, has provided Margaret with money and forces for an anti-Yorkist expedition. Second, as a result of the public humiliation, the once-Yorkist commander Warwicke has switched sides and is now leading the Lancastrians. Yorkist King Edward is taken prisoner, and the following is his new wife's very shrewd assessment of the danger to herself and her immediate family.

Style: as part of a two-handed scene

Where: the palace, in London

To Whom: her brother, Earl Rivers

# of Lines: 27

Probable Timing: 1.20 minutes

Take Note: While most modern texts suggest Elizabeth is well in control of herself throughout, F's orthography and sentence structure show the early cracks and developing uneasiness that build toward the end of the speech, even though she manages to re-establish some momentary calm until the last line and a half.

Queen Elizabeth

1   Why, brother Rivers, are you yet to learn
     What late misfortune is befall'n King Edward ? {-}

     {†} the loss of his own royal person .

2   {He is} almost slain , for he is taken prisoner,
     Either betray'd by falsehood of his guard
     Or by his foe surpris'd at unawares:
     And as I further have to understand,
     Is new committed to the Bishop of York ,
     Fell Warwick's brother, and by that our foe .

3   And I {must †} [wean] me from despair
     For love of Edward's offspring in my womb .

4   This is it that makes me bridle passion,
     And bear with mildness my misfortunes cross ;
     {Ay , ay }, for this I draw in many a tear ,
     And stop the rising of blood-sucking sighs ,
     [Lest] with my sighs or tears I blast or drown
     King Edward's fruit , true heir to th'English crown .

5   {Warwick } I am inform'd {†}comes towards London
     To set the crown once more on Henry's head .

6   Guess thou the rest ; King Edward's friends must down .

7   But to prevent the tyrant's violence
     (For trust not him that hath once broken faith),
     I'll hence forthwith unto the sanctuary,
     To save, at least, the heir of Edward's right ;
     There shall I rest secure from force and fraud .

8   Come therefore, let us fly while we may fly ,
     If Warwick take us we are sure to die .

{Queene Elizabeth} Gray

1   Why Brother Rivers, are you yet to learne
   What late misfortune is befalne King Edward? {-}

{†} the losse of his owne Royall person .

2   {He is} almost slaine, for he is taken prisoner,
   Either betrayd by falshood of his Guard,
   Or by his Foe surpriz'd at unawares:
   And as I further have to understand,
   Is new committed to the Bishop of Yorke,
   Fell Warwickes Brother, and by that our Foe .

3   And I {must †} [waine] me from dispaire
   For love of Edwards Off-spring in my wombe :
   This is it that makes me bridle passion,
   And beare with Mildnesse my misfortunes crosse :
   {I, I}, for this I draw in many a teare,
   And stop the rising of blood-sucking sighes,
   [Least] with my sighes or teares, I blast or drowne
   King Edwards Fruite, true heyre to th'English Crowne .

4   {Warwicke} I am inform'd {†}comes towards London,
   To set the Crowne once more on Henries head,
   Guesse thou the rest, King Edwards Friends must downe .

5   But to prevent the Tyrants violence,
   (For trust not him that hath once broken Faith)
   Ile hence forthwith unto the Sanctuary,
   To save (at least) the heire of Edwards right :
   There shall I rest secure from force and fraud :
   Come therefore let us flye, while we may flye,
   If Warwicke take us, we are sure to dye .

- the recent strain on her is wonderfully highlighted by the only surround phrase in the speech as she envisages taking sanctuary will save not only herself but also Edward's unborn child, ' : There shall I rest secure from force and fraud : ', especially considering that the phrase is also un-embellished (the fifth line of F #5)

- F #1 oscillates between the opening intellect (4/2 in the first two lines) to a sudden emotional flash as she tells her brother that her husband is lost (1/3 in F #1's last line)

- then in F2, elaborating on how her husband was lost and his current whereabouts, she manages to restore some mental discipline (7/3, with two of the long spellings creeping in during the last two lines as she names those who have him)

- despite suggesting that her pregnancy must force her to stay calm (F #3), of the eight lines, the first seven give way to her personal feelings (3/10), while passion swamps the last line (5/3 in eight words!)

- and here F's sentence structure deviates quite markedly from what most modern texts set, for F's remaining onrush is gutted, with F #3 being set as mt. #3 and #4; F #4 as mt. #5 and #6; and F #5 as mt. #7 and #8: thus while F seems to set more immediacy and even urgency, the grammatical tidying of most modern texts seems to set a woman in full analytical mode

- in her analysis of what Warwicke's next move the p assion ending the longer F #3 continues (3/3 in all but the last half line of F #4)

- while she is only too clear (3/1) on what doom it will bring to her family and friends (the last half-line of F #4)

- in planning her retreat to sanctuary she maintains her mental discipline (the first four lines of F #5), yet after the unembellished fifth line hope to avoid 'force and fraud', emotion breaks through once more in the final two line exhortation to flee (1/4), accompanied by two extra commas not set by the modern texts, suggesting perhaps either great urgency or panic at the very end.

The Third Part of Henry the Sixt

Queen/Queene {Margaret}

Oh Ned, sweet Ned, speake to thy Mother Boy .
5.5.51–67

Background: Margaret and her son, the young Prince of Wales, have been captured. As proud as his mother, Ned (a corruption of his given name) has refused to bend to the three Yorkist brothers, insisting that King Edward should 'Speake like a subject, prowd ambitious Yorke', telling them they are 'all undutifull', finishing with 'I am your better, Traytors as ye are,/And thou usurp'st my Fathers right and mine'. All three brothers, Edward, George and Richard stab him to death (just as earlier the Lancastrian Clifford stabbed their youngest brother Rutland). This is Margaret's response.

Style: as part of a five-handed scene, in front of a larger group

Where: the battlefield

To Whom: her dead son and the three Yorkist brothers, in front of the Yorkist forces

# of Lines: 17

Probable Timing: 1.00 minutes

Take Note: While the speech essentially speaks for itself, F adds more details of where and how Margaret gives in and recovers from the appalling event of witnessing the cold-blooded murder of her son.

Queen

1   O Ned, sweet Ned, speak to thy mother, boy !

2   Canst thou not speak ?

3   O traitors, murtherers !

4   They that stabb'd Cæsar shed no blood at all,
    Did not offend, nor were not worthy blame,
    If this foul deed were by to equal it .

5   He was a man ; this, in respect, a child ,
    And men, ne're spend their fury on a child .

6   What's worse [than] murtherer, that I may name it ?

7   No, no, my heart will burst and if I speak ,
    And I will speak , that so my heart may burst .

8   Butchers and villains ! bloody cannibals !
    How sweet a plant have you untimely cropp'd !

9   You have no children, butchers, if you had,
    The thought of them would have stirr'd up remorse,
    But if you ever chance to have a child ,
    Look in his youth to have him so cut off
    As deathsmen, you have rid this sweet young prince !

Queene

1 Oh Ned, sweet Ned, speake to thy Mother Boy .

2 Can'st thou not speake?

3   O Traitors, Murtherers !

4 They that stabb'd Cæsar, shed no blood at all :
   Did not offend, nor were not worthy Blame,
   If this foule deed were by, to equall it .

5 He was a Man ; this (in respect) a Childe,
   And Men, ne're spend their fury on a Childe .

6 What's worse [then] Murtherer, that I may name it ?

7 No, no, my heart will burst, and if I speake,
   And I will speake, that so my heart may burst .

8 Butchers and Villaines, bloudy Caniballes,
   How sweet a Plant have you untimely cropt :
   You have no children (Butchers) if you had,
   The thought of them would have stirr'd up remorse,
   But if you ever chance to have a Childe,
   Looke in his youth to have him so cut off .

9 As deathsmen you have rid this sweet yong Prince .

- F's unusual three short sentence opening points to the enormity of the moment, enhanced as they are by three switches in vocal energy in just two lines—an inordinately passionate F #1 (4/2), an almost neutral F #2 (0/1), followed by pure intellectual hate on the F# 3 attack, (2/0)

- the surround phrases ' . They that stabb'd Cæsar, shed no blood at al : ' and ' . He was a Man ; ' is the basis for her attack on the murderers' lack of manhood

- and as the attack continues, so, with two small exceptions, her passion remains steadfast throughout (14—if 'Butchers' at the start of F #8 is included—/11 in the remaining 15 lines)

- her rhetorical cracks are tiny but telling, such as

  a. the three extra breath-thoughts (two in F #4 and one in #7), as if she needs the extra breaths to be able to make her feelings clear

  b. the onrush of F #8 (placing a curse on any children the murderers may eventually have), the ferocity of which modern texts reduce by splitting it in two

  c. the ungrammatical ending to F #8 separating the final line as an independent sentence (F #9), while syntactically appalling, emphasises her final fury—enhanced by the fact that, save for the capitalisation of 'Prince' (and its painfully fascinating that here she cannot refer to her dead child by name), the short line is unembellished

The Tragedy of Richard the Third

Anne

What do you tremble ? are you all affraid ?

between 1.2.43–67

Background: Anne is about to leave with the hearse, but Richard has challenged the men accompanying her to stop in their tracks, and, after token resistance they have obeyed. This is Anne's response to the man she regards as a double murderer. One note; her reference to Richard as the 'Divell' should not be dismissed as mere hyperbole; this could be a genuine belief, and fueled when Henry's body begins to bleed—since legend has it that such bleeding was only supposed to occur when the body was in the presence of the murderer or the devil himself.

Style: initially to a small group, and then to one person in front of them

Where: a street in London

To Whom: initially the guards and pall bearers, then Richard for them to hear

# of Lines: 24

Probable Timing: 1.15 minutes

Take Note: Whereas Lady Anne was able to retain some degree of composure before Richard, now the 'Foule Divell confronts her, her composure is not quite so easy to maintain (25/24).

Anne

1 What do you tremble ?are you all afraid ?

2 Alas, I blame you not, for you are mortal ,
   And mortal eyes cannot endure the devil .

3 Avaunt , thou dreadful minister of hell !

4 Thou hadst but power over his mortal body,
   His soul thou canst not have . {†}

5 Foul devil , for God's sake hence, and trouble us not,
   For thou hast made the happy earth thy hell,
   Fill'd it with cursing cries and deep exclaims .

6 If thou delight to view thy heinous deeds,
   Behold this pattern of thy butcheries .

7 O gentlemen, see, see dead Henry's wounds
   Open their congeal'd mouths and bleed afresh !

8 Blush, blush, thou lump of foul deformity ;
   For 'tis thy presence that exhales this blood
   From cold and empty veins where no blood dwells .

9 Thy [deed inhuman] and unnatural
   Provokes this deluge most unnatural .

10 O God !which this blood mad'st, revenge his death !
    O Earth !which this blood drink'st, revenge his death !

11 Either heav'n with lightning strike thee murth'rer dead ;
    Or earth gape open wide and eat him quick ,
    As thou dost swallow up this good King's blood,
    Which his hell-govern'd arm hath butchered !

Anne

1   What do you tremble ?are you all affraid ?

2   Alas, I blame you not, for you are Mortall,
And Mortall eyes cannot endure the Divell .

3   Avant thou dreadfull minister of Hell ;
Thou had'st but power over his Mortall body,
His Soule thou canst not have . {†}

---

4   Foule Divell,°
For Gods sake hence, and trouble us not,
For thou hast made the happy earth thy Hell :
Fill'd it with cursing cries, and deepe exclaimes :
If thou delight to view thy heynous deeds,
Behold this patterne of thy Butcheries .

5   Oh Gentlemen, see, see dead Henries wounds,
Open their congeal'd mouthes, and bleed afresh .

6   Blush, blush, thou lumpe of fowle Deformitie :
For 'tis thy presence that exhales this blood
From cold and empty Veines where no blood dwels .

7   Thy [Deeds inhumane] and unnaturall,
Provokes this Deluge most unnaturall .

8   O God !which this Blood mad'st, revenge his death :
O Earth !which this Blood drink'st, revenge his death .

9   Either Heav'n with Lightning strike thee murth'rer dead :
Or Earth gape open wide, and eate him quicke,
As thou dost swallow up this good Kings blood,
Which his Hell-govern'd arme hath butchered .

- the surround phrases, especially the first formed by the only (emotional) semicolon in the speech, begin to explain why, first in terms of what he represents

    " . Avant, thou dreadfull minister of Hell ; "
  then his effect on England

      " Fill'd it with cursing cries, and deepe exclaimes : "
  leading to the curse

    " . O God ! Which this Blood mad'st, revenge his death: /O Earth
        ! Which this Blood drink'st, revenge his death ."
  and her wish that

    " . Either Heav'n with Lightning strike thee murth'rer dead : "

- the onrush of both sentence #3 and #4 suggest that standing up to Richard is not as easy as most modern texts suggest, for they reduce much of the onrush by splitting both sentences in two

- the difficulty is even more marked at the start of F #4, which opens with a split line, as if it is initially awkward for her to begin: most modern texts set the two parts of the split line as one

- the depth of her passion is highlighted by the very rare presence in an Elizabethan or Jacobean text of two exclamation marks (following the second word of each line in F #8), just as she culminates her attack on Richard with her appeal for God's help

- her intellectual composure is only regained at one point in the speech, her appeal to God (6/0 in F #8 and the first line of F #9)

- for the rest of the time, she either is taken over by passion, as she
    a. first faces down Richard (F #1-3 and the first 3 lines of #4, 9/8)
    b. sees Henry's wounds open afresh (F #5-7, 6/8)
    c. asks that the Earth deal with Richard as he dealt with Henry (3/3, the last three lines of F #9)

- or just once taken over by emotion, as she explains how Richard has made the earth his 'Hell' before showing him the body he has butchered (the last three lines of F #4, ¼

The Tragedy of Richard the Third
Queen/Queene Margaret

What ? were you snarling all before I came,
1.3.187–213

Background: Margaret, widow to the murdered King Henry VI, was banished to France. However, she hasn't yet left, and here, spying on the squabbles of the now-rulers of England, the enemy Yorkists, she has burst in on them to add her voice to the already fever-pitch accusations. One note; apart from King Edward, whose memory plays no part in this speech, there are two other distinct Edwards referred to— the first Edward, Margaret's son, was killed by the Yorkists at the end of the companion play, *Henry the Sixt Part Three*; the second Edward is the still-alive heir presumptive to the throne, the oldest child of King Edward and Elizabeth (a child Richard will kill later in this play).

Style: group address

Where: the palace

To Whom: the Queene, her brother Rivers and sons Gray and Dorset, Richard, and the nobles Buckingham, Derby, and Hastings: most modern texts suggest that sentences #6-8 are spoken directly to Elizabeth

# of Lines: 27

Probable Timing: 1.20 minutes

Take Note: F's orthography suggests an unexpected opening and closing for Margaret; and, compared to how she curses out everyone else, she employs a very different form of attack on Elizabeth, now an ex-Queene herself, the woman who once took the throne from Margaret.

Background

Queen Margaret

1   What ?were you snarling all before I came,
    Ready to catch each other by the throat,
    And turn you all your hatred now on me ?

2   Did York's dread curse prevail so much with heaven
    That Henry's death, my lovely Edward's death,
    Their kingdom's loss , my woeful banishment,
    Should all but answer for that peevish brat ?

3   Can curses pierce the clouds and enter heaven ?

4   Why then give way, dull clouds, to my quick curses !

5   Though not by war , by surfeit die your king,
    As ours by murther, to make him a king !

6   Edward thy son , that now is Prince of Wales,
    For Edward [my] son , that was Prince of Wales,
    Die in his youth by like untimely violence !

7   Thyself a queen , for me that was a queen ,
    Out-live thy glory like my wretched self !

8   Long mayst thou live, to wail thy children's death,
    And see another, as I see thee now,
    Deck'd in thy rights as thou art stall'd in mine !

9   Long die thy happy days before thy death,
    And after many length'ned hours of grief ,
    Die neither mother, wife, nor England's queen !

10 Rivers and Dorset, you were standers-°by,
    And so wast thou, Lord Hastings, when my son
    Was stabb'd with bloody daggers : God, I pray him
    That none of you may live his natural age,
    But by some unlook'd accident cut off !

Queene Margaret

1   What ?were you snarling all before I came,
    Ready to catch each other by the throat,
    And turne you all your hatred now on me ?

2   Did Yorkes dread Curse prevaile so much with Heaven,
    That Henries death, my lovely Edwards death,
    Their Kingdomes losse, my wofull Banishment,
    Should all but answer for that peevish Brat ?

3   Can Curses pierce the Clouds, and enter Heaven ?

4   Why then give way dull Clouds to my quick Curses .

5   Though not by Warre, by Surfet dye your King,
    As ours by Murther, to make him a King .

6   Edward thy Sonne, that now is Prince of Wales,
    For Edward [our] Sonne, that was Prince of Wales,
    Dye in his youth, by like untimely violence .

7   Thy selfe a Queene, for me that was a Queene,
    Out-live thy glory, like my wretched selfe :
    Long may'st thou live, to wayle thy Childrens death,
    And see another, as I see thee now,
    Deck'd in thy Rights, as thou art stall'd in mine .

8   Long dye thy happie dayes, before thy death,
    And after many length'ned howres of griefe,
    Dye neyther Mother, Wife, nor Englands Queene .

9   Rivers and Dorset, you were standers by,
    And so wast thou, Lord Hastings, when my Sonne
    Was stab'd with bloody Daggers :God, I pray him,
    That none of you may live his naturall age,
    But by some unlook'd accident cut off .

- for such a destructive speech, F #1 starts out very carefully (0/1), with
the first two lines non-embellished, almost as if she is drawing power
to calm herself from their dissention

- as she recalls the devastating effect the curse of her old nemesis Yorke
wrought on her and her family, all stemming from her murder of
Yorke's youngest son, her passion is fully released (8/4, F #2)

- though her mind comes to the fore with the notion that if Yorke's
curse worked, why shouldn't hers (5/0 in two lines), the discovery is
not necessarily rational, for it takes two short F sentences (F#3-4),
the second much faster without the added modern commas, to for-
mulate such a bizarre idea

- and as she begins her curse, starting with Edward and his children, so
her intellect is given full rein (13/5 in just the five lines of F #5-6)

- but as she begins to attack the woman who replaced her as Queen,
her emotions sweep back in, and then build: the onrushed start
maintains an almost equal balance of intellect and emotion (4/5 in
the five lines of F #7); however, the passion of her sustained drive is
somewhat reduced by most modern texts that split the sentence in
two and create a more controlled Margaret than F originally set

- the development of the attack on the Queen then spills into more of
an emotional release (4/7 in the three lines of F #8)

- the attack on her rival finished, Margaret manages to revert to mental discipline in the still-vehement attack on the 'standers by' (6/1 in
the first two and a half lines of F #9)

- and then, as with the start of the speech, she seems to regain a state
of calm (or perhaps exhaustion) for her (final) appeal for God's help
(1/1 in a line and a half), with a final non-embellished line of a dreadful curse 'But by some unlook'd accident cut off.'

The Tragedy of Richard the Third
Queen/Queene Margaret

Stay Dog, for ÿ shalt heare me .
1.3.215–232

Background: Following up on the prior speech, she now turns her attention to the about to depart Richard. Note that the last line breaks off because Richard interrupts her .

Style: one on one address in front of a larger group

Where: the palace

To Whom: Richard, in front of the current queen Elizabeth, her brother Rivers and sons Gray and Dorset, the nobles Buckingham, Derby, and Hastings

# of Lines: 18

Probable Timing: 0.55 minutes

Take Note: Often referred to as 'mad Margaret', F's sentence structure and, here especially, orthography, shows why—for she is nowhere near as rational as modern texts suggest.

Queen Margaret

1 {†} Stay, dog, for [thou] shalt hear me .

2 If heaven have any grievous plague in store
Exceeding those that I can wish upon thee,
O, let them keep it till thy sins be ripe,
And then hurl down their indignation
On thee, the troubler of the poor world's peace !

3 The worm of conscience still begnaw thy soul !

4 Thy friends suspect for traitors while thou liv'st,
And take deep traitors for thy dearest friends !

5 No sleep close up that deadly eye of thine,
Unless it be while some tormenting dream
Affrights thee with a hell of ugly devils !

6 Thou elvish-°mark'd, abortive, rooting hog !
Thou that wast seal'd in thy nativity
The slave of nature and the son of hell !
Thou slander of thy heavy mother's womb !
Thou loathed issue of thy father's loins !
Thou rag of honor, thou detested—

Queene Margaret

1 {†} {S}tay Dog, for [ÿ] shalt heare me .

2   If Heaven have any grievous plague in store,
Exceeding those that I can wish upon thee,
O let them keepe it, till thy sinnes be ripe,
And then hurle downe their indignation
On thee, the troubler of the poore Worlds peace .

3   The Worme of Conscience still begnaw thy Soule,
Thy Friends suspect for Traytors while thou liv'st,
And take deepe Traytors for thy dearest Friends :
No sleepe close up that deadly Eye of thine,
Unlesse it be while some tormenting Dreame
Affrights thee with a Hell of ougly Devills .

4   Thou elvish mark'd, abortive rooting Hogge,
Thou that wast seal'd in thy Nativitie
The slave of Nature, and the Sonne of Hell :
Thou slander of thy heavie Mothers Wombe,
Thou loathed Issue of thy Fathers Loynes,
Thou Ragge of Honor, thou detested—

- the opening short (half-line) passionate sentence (1/1), minus the extra comma most modern texts add suggests she is extraordinarily vulnerable emotionally and mentally

- as she calls on heaven's help (F #2) so her emotion gets the better of her (2/5)

- the onrush of F #3, as the highly concentrated details of her curse on him turns into high passion (11/10 in six lines), is highly reduced by most modern texts splitting the sentence into three

- and as she turns her invective onto Richard himself and his family, mental discipline finally asserts itself very strongly, underscoring the strength of her belief (12/5 in the six lines of F #4)

- in addition to sentence restructuring, many modern texts create more certainty in her by adding eight exclamation points not set in F1: several of them turn what is speed in F (piling detail on detail via commas) into deliberate moments of release (see lines 1, 3, 4 and 5 of mt. #6 and compare the line-ending punctuation set there to those of F #4 at the same spot)

The Tragedy of Richard the Third
Duchess/Dutchesse

I prythee heare me speake .
between 4.4.180–196

Background: though Richard's mother, the Dutchesse of Yorke has
been outspoken against him from the start of the play, and with
each murder—of his family; loyalists; and supporters (including
his wife Lady Anne, and Hastings); and his own flesh and blood
(his brother, her son Clarence, and her grandchildren—Edward's
children, the Princes in the Tower)—her pain and loathing has
grown exponentially. The following self explanatory speech con-
tains her final words to him and in the play.

Style: one on one in front of a small group

Where: unspecified, perhaps a street near the Tower, or at the palace

To Whom: Richard, in front of Elizabeth, mother of 'Edwards
Children' (sentence #5), Catesby, and Richard's military 'traine'

# of Lines: 16

Probable Timing: 0.50 minutes

Take Note: As she faces her son for the last time, and adds her curses
to those of many other characters in the play, so F1's orthography
shows a journey from the highly personal to the intellectual.

Duchess

1   I prithee hear me speak .

___

2   Hear me a word ;
    For I shall never speak to thee again .

___

3   Either thou wilt die by God's just ordinance
    Ere from this war thou turn a conqueror,
    Or I with grief and extreme age shall perish
    And never more behold thy face again .

4   Therefore take with thee my most grievous curse,
    Which in the day of battle tire thee more
    [Than] all the complete armor that thou wear'st !

5   My prayers on the adverse party fight,
    And there the little souls of Edward's children
    Whisper the spirits of thine enemies
    And promise them success and victory .

6   Bloody thou art, bloody will be thy end ;
    Shame serves thy life, and doth thy death attend .

Dutchesse

1   I prythee heare me speake .

---

2   Heare me a word :
     For I shall never speake to thee againe .

---

3   Either thou wilt dye, by Gods just ordinance
     Ere from this warre thou turne a Conqueror :
     Or I with greefe and extreame Age shall perish,
     And never more behold thy face againe .

4   Therefore take with thee my most greevous Curse,
     Which in the day of Battell tyre thee more
     [Then] all the compleat Armour that thou wear'st .

5   My Prayers on the adverse party fight,
     And there the little soules of Edwards Children,
     Whisper the Spirits of thine Enemies,
     And promise them Successe and Victory :
     Bloody thou art, bloody will be thy end :
     Shame serves thy life, and doth thy death attend .

- the opening short sentence shows how difficult the following is going to be for her; indeed her opening is totally emotional (0/6, F #1-2)

- the four surround phrases show the importance of her action and the basis of her contempt

  " . Heare me a word : /For I shall never speake to thee againe . "

  and especially the final naked bare-bones appalling non-embellished summation of her last remaining son

  " : Bloody thou art, bloody will be thy end : /Shame serves thy life, and doth thy death attend . "

- as the curse starts (F #3-4), some element of mental control is seen though emotion still predominates (6/11)

- but as she spells out just how far she intends her curse to go – to the extent of praying for victory for the forces opposed to Richard – so a ferocious intellect takes over (7/2 in the first four lines of F #5), and this together with the two extra commas suggest she is taking great care that every point she makes strikes home

- that she can finish so calmly (the last two lines are non-embellished) suggests that the bleak recognition of her son's evil knows no bounds

The Tragedy of Richard the Third
Queen/Queene {Elizabeth}
My Babes were destin'd to a fairer death,
between 4.4.220–235

Background: having discarded, i.e. killed, his first politically advan-
tageous wife (Lady Anne), Richard now needs to both bolster up
his own claim to the throne and prevent the new claimant, Henry
Earl of Richmond, from bolstering his. Richard believes his only
recourse is to marry his niece, daughter of his older brother the
once King Edward, niece to Clarence whom he killed, and sister to
the two Princes in the Tower, whom he also had killed (not forget-
ting that he also killed her mother's brother—Rivers—and son by
her first marriage—Gray). The situation is urgent, for Richmond
is seeking to marry her too. At the top of speech Richard has only
just begun the delicate and seemingly impossible negotiations with
her mother, the woman he has detested and plotted against for so
long, the ex-Queen Elizabeth, when she begins her counter attack,
starting with the death of her sons, the two young Princes

Style: part of a two-handed scene, perhaps in front of a small group

Where: unspecified, perhaps a street near the Tower, or at the palace

To Whom: Richard, perhaps in front of Catesby and Richard's military 'traine'

# of Lines: 15

Probable Timing: 0.50 minutes

Queen

1   My babes were destin'd to a fairer death,
     If grace had blest thee with a fairer life .

---

2   Cousins {†}, by their uncle cozen'd
     Of comfort, kingdom , kindred, freedom , life.

3   Whose hand soever [lanc'd] their tender hearts,
     Thy head (all indirectly) gave direction .

4   No doubt the murd'rous knife was dull and blunt
     Till it was whetted on thy stone-hard heart
     To revel in the entrails of my lambs .

5   But that still use of grief makes wild grief tame,
     My tongue should to thy ears not name my boys
     Till that my nails were anchor'd in thine eyes ;
     And I, in such a desp'rate bay of death,
     Like a poor bark of sails and tackling reft,
     Rush all to pieces on thy rocky bosom .

Queene

1 My Babes were destin'd to a fairer death,
   If grace had blest thee with a fairer life .

---

2 Cosins {†}, by their Unckle couzend,
   Of Comfort, Kingdome, Kindred, Freedome, Life,
   Whose hand soever [lanch'd] their tender hearts,
   Thy head (all indirectly) gave direction .

3 No doubt the murd'rous Knife was dull and blunt,
   Till it was whetted on thy stone-hard heart,
   To revell in the Intrailes of my Lambes .

4 But that still use of greefe, makes wilde greefe tame,
   My tongue should to thy eares not name my Boyes,
   Till that my Nayles were anchor'd in thine eyes :
   And I in such a desp'rate Bay of death,
   Like a poore Barke, of sailes and tackling reft,
   Rush all to peeces on thy Rocky bosome .

- there are moments of (enforced?) non-embellished calm where she lays her soul bare: initially they are accusatory and come at the end of sentences 'If grace had blest thee with a fairer life' (F #1), and 'Whose hand soever lanch'd their tender hearts,/Thy head (all indirectly) gave direction.' (F #2) as if she were trying very hard to maintain control so as not to be accused of hysteria

- but, as the speech develops, it seems that she cannot maintain control, for the final non-embellished, and more personal, attack comes in the middle of F #3, 'Till it was whetted on they stone-hard heart,'

- and it is at this point that four of F's six extra breath-thoughts are clustered, perhaps suggesting Elizabeth is still trying to ensure that every point she makes strikes home before high-excess (twenty-one releases in just seven lines) sweeps in to finish the speech

- while at first the speech seems to build carefully, F #1's careful in-tellect (1/0) leads to a quick outburst of passion (6/4 in the first two lines of F #2) that is equally quickly controlled (1/0 for the next four lines until the last line of F #3)

- suddenly all control is lost, for as she speaks of the butchering of her boys at the end of F #3 and the beginning of #4, and as to how grief from that butchery will help her now, there is a passionate outburst in just two lines (2/6), while the talk of herself physically attacking Richard (the last five lines of the speech) releases passion in her once more (more emotional than intellectual, 5/8)

The Tragedy of Richard the Third
Queen/Queene {Elizabeth}

My daughters Mother thinkes it with her soule,
between 4.4.257–284

Background: Following up on the prior speech, this speech is
Elizabeth's response to Richard's continued expression of love for
her daughter, culminating in 'Then know,/That from my Soule, I
love thy Daughter'

Style: each as part of a two-handed scene, perhaps in front of a small
group

Where: unspecified, perhaps a street near the Tower, or at the palace

To Whom: Richard, perhaps in front of Catesby and Richard's military 'traine'

# of Lines: 21

Probable Timing: 1.05 minutes

Queen

1   My daughter's mother thinks it with her soul {,}

                           ———————————————————————

     That thou dost love my daughter from thy soul ;
     So from thy souls love didst thou love her brothers,
     And from my hearts love I do thank thee for it .

2   How canst thou woo her ?

     ———————————————————————

3   {†}   {W}ilt thou learn of me ?

     ———————————————————————

4   Send to her by the man that slew her brothers
     A pair of bleeding hearts ;thereon engrave
     "Edward" and "York" ;then haply will she weep .

5   Therefore present to her—as [sometimes] Margaret
     Did to thy father, steep'd in Rutland's blood -
     A hand°kerchief , which, say to her, did drain
     The purple sap from her sweet brother's body,
     And bid her wipe her weeping eyes withal .

6   If this inducement move her not to love,
     Send her a letter of thy noble deeds :
     Tell her thou mad'st away her uncle Clarence,
     Her uncle Rivers, ay (and for her sake !),
     Mad'st quick conveyance with her good Aunt Anne .

     ———————————————————————

7   There is no other way,
     Unless thou couldst put on some other shape
     And not be Richard that hath done all this .

Queene

1 My daughters Mother thinkes it with her soule {,}

That thou dost love my daughter from thy soule
So from thy Soules love didst thou love her Brothers,
And from my hearts love, I do thanke thee for it .

2 How canst thou woo her ?

3 {†}   {W}ilt thou learne of me ?

4 Send to her by the man that slew her Brothers,
A paire of bleeding hearts : thereon ingrave
Edward and Yorke, then haply will she weepe :
Therefore present to her, as [sometime] Margaret
Did to thy Father, steept in Rutlands blood,
A hand-kercheefe, which say to her did dreyne
The purple sappe from her sweet Brothers body,
And bid her wipe her weeping eyes withall .

5 If this inducement move her not to love,
Send her a Letter of thy Noble deeds :
Tell her, thou mad'st away her Unckle Clarence,
Her Unckle Rivers, I (and for her sake)
Mad'st quicke conveyance with her good Aunt Anne .

6 There is no other way,
Unlesse thou could'st put on some other shape,
And not be Richard, that hath done all this .

- a combination of non-embellished lines and surround phrases clearly establishes the well of pain and anger from which this speech springs, viz.

  "How canst thou woo her?",

  plus the two surround phrases

  " . Send to her by the man that slew her Brothers,/A paire of bleeding hearts : thereon ingrave Edward and Yorke,/ then haply will she weepe : "

  plus the non-embellished lines

  "If this inducement move her not to love,", and "There is no other way,"

- the strain that she is undergoing can be seen in the springing through from line two to line three without any punctuation, while most modern texts remove the evidence of strain by ending the line with a semicolon

- and her early strain also manifests itself in F's two unusual short sentences (#2-3) which might suggest that, after the passionate opening (F #1, 3/5), she is bracing herself for what is to come

- for after the equally passionate start to F #4 (3/3 in the first three lines), and as she (ironically) begins to list a possible approach, so her intellect takes over for the next two lines, comparing what he should do with what Margaret did to his brother (3/0), but this cannot be maintained, for the details of that child murder move the Queene to emotion (1/4 in the last three lines)

- but then she returns to her ironic suggestions, and does so with tremendous intellectual gusto (8/3, F #5)

- while the return to a serious finish is marked by a somewhat calmer approach (1/1 in the two and a half lines of F #6), it is partly created by two extra breath- thoughts, an attempt to ensure that she stays calm so that her final derogatory stripping of Richard is fully understood

The Life and Death of King John
Eleanor/Old Queene

Son, list to this conjunction, make this match

2.1.468–479

Background: the following is the response of John's mother (Eleanor), a superb political assessment of the current situation and Hubert's suggestion for resolving the current military impasse.

Style: part of a two handed scene in front of a larger group

Where: outside Angiers

To Whom: King John of England, in front of his niece Blanche, Philip the Bastard, and English forces; King Philip of France, his son Lewis the Dolphin, and French forces; Lymoges, Duke of Austria; French and English Heralds

# of Lines: 12

Probable Timing: 0.40 minutes

Take Note: The reason for the politically astute advice from the Old Queene (Eleanor, John's mother) is clearly seen in the one surround phrase, " . I see a yeelding in the lookes of France : "

Queen Eleanor

1   Son, list to this conjunction, make this match,
     Give with our niece a dowry large enough,
     For by this knot thou shalt so surely tie
     Thy now unsur'd assurance to the crown ,
     That yon green boy shall have no sun to ripe
     The bloom that promiseth a mighty fruit .

2   I see a yielding in the looks of France ;
     Mark how they whisper .

3   Urge them while their souls
     Are capable of this ambition,
     [Lest] zeal , now melted by the windy breath
     Of soft petitions, pity , and remorse,
     Cool and congeal again to what it was .

Old Queene

1   Son, list to this conjunction, make this match
Give with our Neece a dowrie large enough,
For by this knot, thou shalt so surely tye
Thy now unsur'd assurance to the Crowne,
That yon greene boy shall have no Sunne to ripe
The bloome that promiseth a mightie fruite .

2   I see a yeelding in the lookes of France :
Marke how they whisper, urge them while their soules
Are capeable of this ambition,
[Least] zeale now melted by the windie breath
Of soft petitions, pittie and remorse,
Coole and congeale againe to what it was .

- the single extra breath-thought in F #1, line 3, is again testament to her political acumen, for it pinpoints exactly what John has to gain by agreeing to the marriage, viz. 'thou shalt surely tye'

- that she can think fast on her feet can be deduced

  a. once the unnecessary modern text added commas are removed from the first line of F #1 and lines 4-5 of F #2

  b. and in the onrush of F #2 moving within the same sentence from noticing France's potential yielding to immediate advice, suggesting a political artist capable of making very quick decisions: modern texts set the noticing as mt. #2, and the advice (mt. #3) as shown, making the speech rather predictable and rational in comparison to F 's more spontaneous shrewdness

- thus it's not surprising that the speech is almost totally full of personal release (3/18)

The Life and Death of King John
Constance

A wicked day, and not a holy day .
3.1.83–95

Background: with all the wedding, and therefore peace-signing, cele-
brants having come from the ceremony, they are faced with a right-
fully upset Constance, whose following speech is triggered by the
King of France's comment to his new daughter-in-law Blanche 'Tis
true (faire daughter) and this blessed day,/Ever in France shall be
kept festivall:/ . . . /The yearely course that brings this day about,/
Shall never see it, but a holy day'.

Style: a group address for the benefit of all present

Where: in or just outside Angiers

To Whom: King John of England, Eleanor, the Bastard, Blanche;
King Philip of France, the Dolphin, Austria; Arthur; plus others
from both sides, including Salisbury

# of Lines: 13

Probable Timing: 0.45 minutes

Take Note: This speech is remarkably (and deceptively) calm.

Constance

1   A wicked day, and not a holy day !

2   What hath this day deserv'd? what hath it done,
     That it in golden letters should be set
     Among the high tides in the calendar ?

3   Nay, rather turn this day out of the week ,
     This day of shame, oppression, perjury .

4   Or if it must stand still, let wives with child
     Pray that their burthens may not fall this day,
     Lest that their hopes prodigiously be cross'd ;
     But on this day let sea°men fear no wrack ;
     No bargains break that are not this day made :
     This day all things begun come to ill end,
     Yea, faith itself to hollow falsehood change !

Constance

1   A wicked day, and not a holy day .

2   What hath this day deserv'd? what hath it done,
That it in golden letters should be set
Among the high tides in the Kalender?

3   Nay, rather turne this day out of the weeke,
This day of shame, oppression, perjury .

4   Or if it must stand still, let wives with childe
Pray that their burthens may not fall this day,
Lest that their hopes prodigiously be crost :
But (on this day) let Sea-men feare no wracke,
No bargaines breake that are not this day made ;
This day all things begun, come to ill end,
Yea, faith it selfe to hollow falshood change .

- the four lines of F's opening two sentences are very calm (probably enforced) with just one capital letter in the last line of F #2

- which leads to two emotional words in the following line, as if an explosion was about to start

- but, for a moment, Constance seems to re-establish control, for there's only one more excess ('childe') in the next four lines, but she cannot contain herself further

- for following the colon, compared to the rest of the speech, she finally explodes emotionally (1/5) as she begins to curse the day for now and for all the years to come

- the non-embellished lines (#1-3; #6; #8-9; #12) outline the thoughts that are seething within her

The Life and Death of King John
Constance

You have beguil'd me with a counterfeit
3.1.99–112

Background: the following comes immediately after previous speech, and is triggered by what proves to be the King of France's empty claim 'By heaven Lady, you shall have no cause/To curse the faire proceedings of this day:/Have I not pawn'd to you my Majesty'.

Style: to one man, and then the gods in general;

Where: in or just outside Angiers

To Whom: initially to King Philip of France

# of Lines: 14

Probable Timing: 0.45 minutes

Take Note: The disintegration of Constance's personal calm seen towards the end of the previous speech continues, and F's orthography and sentence structure show, how slowly at first but then ever more quickly, the dam of self-control gives way.

Constance

1   You have beguil'd me with a counterfeit
    Resembling majesty, which being touch'd and tried ,
    Proves valueless .

2   You are forsworn , forsworn !

3   You came in arms to spill mine enemies blood ,
    But now in arms you strengthen it with yours .

4   The grappling vigor and rough frown of war
    Is [cool'd] in amity and painted peace,
    And our oppression hath made up this league .

5   Arm , arm , you heavens, against these perjur'd kings !

6   A widow cries; be husband to me, heavens!

7   Let not the hours of this ungodly day
    Wear out the [day] in peace ; but ere sun°set,
    Set armed discord 'twixt these perjur'd kings!

8   Hear me, O , hear me !

Constance

1   You have beguil'd me with a counterfeit
    Resembling Majesty, which being touch'd and tride,
    Proves valuelesse : you are forsworne, forsworne,
    You came in Armes to spill mine enemies bloud,
    But now in Armes, you strengthen it with yours .

2   The grapling vigor, and rough frowne of Warre
    Is [cold] in amitie, and painted peace,
    And our oppression hath made up this league :
    Arme, arme, you heavens, against these perjur'd Kings,
    A widdow cries, be husband to me (heavens)
    Let not the howres of this ungodly day
    Weare out the [daies] in Peace ; but ere Sun-set,
    Set armed discord 'twixt these perjur'd Kings,
    Heare me, Oh, heare me .

- that the strain is beginning to tell can be seen in that while F sets just two onrushed sentences, most modern texts suggest each are highly ungrammatical, and split F #1 into three, and F #2 into five

- F's opening two and a half line general statement of France's and Austria's words being 'valueless' is almost kept in check (1/2), but then begins to break as she calls them out for being 'forsworne' (2/4 in the final two and a half lines of F #1)

- for a moment it seems if she has regained control, for the second and third line of F #2 are non-embellished, but the neutrality of the energy is deceptive, for the images of the kings being 'cold in amitie', offering herself and Arthur 'painted peace' and 'oppression', are so strong that

- in the next three and a half lines, as she appeals to the heavens for help, all passion breaks loose (2/5)

- and the speech finishes with an (emotional) semicolon leading to an intellectual plea for immediate discord (2/0) followed by an emotional final half line of appeal for the heavens to 'heare' her (1/3)

The Life and Death of King John
Constance

War, war, no peace, peace is to me a warre :
3.1.113–129

Background: this speech is her immediate response to Austria's 'Lady Constance, peace'.

Style: to one man—both for all listening

Where: in or just outside Angiers

To Whom: to the Duke of Austria, both speeches in front of King John of England, Eleanor, the Bastard, Blanche; the Dolphin; Arthur; others in attendance from both sides, including Salisbury

# of Lines: 17

Probable Timing: 0.55 minutes

Take Note: F allows Constance's onrush to continue, while most modern texts split F #1 into four, and F#2 and #3 each into two, thus reducing the build of her release. In addition, F's orthography clearly shows where the expected, emotional explosion finally breaks through.

Constance

1   War, war, no peace !

2   Peace is to me a war !

3   O Lymoges, O Austria ! thou dost shame
     That bloody spoil .

4   Thou slave, thou wretch, [thou] coward !
     Thou little valiant, great in villainy !
     Thou ever strong upon the stronger side !
     Thou Fortunes champion, that dost never fight
     But when her humorous ladyship is by
     To teach thee safety ! thou art perjur'd too,
     And sooth'st up greatness .

5   What a fool art thou,
     A ramping fool , to brag and stamp and swear
     Upon my party !

6   ·   Thou cold blooded slave,
     Hast thou not spoke like thunder on my side?
     Been sworn my soldier , bidding me depend
     Upon thy stars , thy fortune, and thy strength,
     And dost thou now fall over to my foes?

7   Thou wear a lions hide !

8   Doff it for shame,
     And hang a calve's-°skin on those recreant limbs .

Constance

1　War, war, no peace, peace is to me a warre :
　O Lymoges, O Austria, thou dost shame
　That bloudy spoyle : thou slave, thou wretch, [ÿ] coward,
　Thou little valiant, great in villanie,
　Thou ever strong upon the stronger side ;
　Thou Fortunes Champion, that do'st never fight
　But when her humourous Ladiship is by
　To teach thee safety : thou art perjur'd too,
　And sooth'st up greatnesse .

2　　　　　　　　　　　　　　　　What a foole art thou,
　A ramping foole, to brag, and stamp, and sweare,
　Upon my partie : thou cold blooded slave,
　Hast thou not spoke like thunder on my side?
　Beene sworne my Souldier, bidding me depend
　Upon thy starres, thy fortune, and thy strength,
　And dost thou now fall over to my foes?

3　Thou weare a Lyons hide, doff it for shame,
　And hang a Calves skin on those recreant limbes .

- the five speech pattern variations in the eight and a half lines of F's opening sentence show just how much is struggling within her

  a. the opening line is barely passionate – until the very last word, where the already twice used 'war' suddenly becomes 'warre'

  b. the one and a half line attempt to shame Austria (also known as Lymoges, who wears a lion skin as proof of his military prowess and courage), is passionate (2/2) the use of his given names notwithstanding

  c. and then her expanded belittling of him (starting 'thou slave…') becomes deadly calm with two and a half lines of non-embellished insults

  d. which leads to two and a half lines of intellectual insult (starting 'Thou Fortunes Champion…', 3/1)

  e. finishing with a surround phrase of dreadful summation of Austria as essentially an ass-licker ' ; thou art perjuur'd too,/And sooth'st up greatnesse . '

- and then she blows, with a sustained emotional assault in the six and a half-lines of F #2 (1/7), and even then two of these lines are non-embellished, summing up his hypocrisy so neatly, 'Hast thou not spoke like thunder on my side?' & 'And dost thou now fall over to my foes?', so really the emotional splurge is in just four and a half of those six and a half lines

- and the diatribe ends passionately (2/3) as she suggests that in his 'shame' his proper attire should be a 'Calves skin' rather than a 'Lyons hide'

The Life and Death of King John
Blanche

Upon thy wedding day?

3.1.300–309

Background: because of John's intransigence in refusing to install the duly appointed Archbishop of Canterbury, and Pandulph's refusal to ease the military demands on France, renewal of the fighting between the French and English seems inevitable. As Constance and her son Arthur have been sacrificed to the manly art of diplomacy, so it now seems that Blanche will be similarly sacrificed for the sake of war. This speech is her response to her new French husband's demand (as son to the King of France) for France to immediately take arms against her English uncle King John.

Style: to one man;

To Whom: to her husband the Dolphin, in front of King John of England, Philip the Bastard, and English forces; King Philip of France, and French forces; Lymoges, Duke of Austria; Constance and her son Arthur; Hubert of Angiers; French and English Heralds

# of Lines: 12

Probable Timing: 0.40 minutes

Take Note: Blanche has already shown how calm and dignified she is in her utterances. In this speech F shows calm in the great strain she is undergoing, and also when her calm surface begins to be disturbed.

Blanche

1   Upon thy wedding day?

2   Against the blood that thou hast married?

3   What, shall our feast be kept with slaughtered men?

4   Shall braying trumpets, and loud churlish drums,
     Clamors of hell, be measures to our pomp?

5   O husband, hear me ! ay , alack , how new
     Is "husband" in my mouth ! even for that name,
     Which till this time my tongue did ne'er pronounce,
     Upon my knee I beg, go not to arms
     Against mine uncle .

---

6   Now shall I see thy love .

7   What motive may
     Be stronger with thee [than] the name of wife?

Blanche

1   Upon thy wedding day?

2   Against the blood that thou hast married?

3   What, shall our feast be kept with slaughtered men?

4   Shall braying trumpets, and loud churlish drums
    Clamors of hell, be measures to our pomp?

5   O husband heare me : aye, alacke, how new
    Is husband in my mouth? even for that name
    Which till this time my tongue did nere pronounce ;
    Upon my knee I beg, goe not to Armes
    Against mine Uncle .

---

6   Now shall I see thy love, what motive may
    Be stronger with thee, [then] the name of wife?

- F opens with a startling sequence of three non-embellished short sentences, and each actress must consider whether this is her natural state or a shocked and enforced calm at how her wedding day is developing

- and while the non-embellishment amazingly continues into F #4, the first ripple might be seen in that without the modern extra comma at the end of line 1, the image of 'drums' as the 'clamors of hell' force her to spill over the end of the line and cram the two images together

- the two surround phrases ' . O husband heare me : ' and ' . Upon my knee I beg, goe not to Armes/against mine Uncle . ' show what is disturbing her, this latter phrase showing the most passionate disturbance in the speech (2/2)

- the only other sign of excess is (for her) an enormously passionate line, which starts with the other surround phrase, opening F #5 (0/3)

- and, amazingly, the speech ends with yet another two unembellished lines as she challenges her new husband to make proof of the value of the marriage

The Life and Death of King John
Blanche

The Sun's orecast with bloud : faire day adieu,
3.1.326–336

Background: Following the prior speech, this speech follows her uncle's equally combative 'France thou shalt rue this houre within this houre'.

Style: solo and to two men, both in front of a larger group

Where: outside Angiers

To Whom: to herself and to her husband the Dolphin and her uncle, King John of England, in front of Philip the Bastard, and English forces; King Philip of France, and French forces; Lymoges, Duke of Austria; Constance and her son Arthur; Hubert of Angiers; French and English Heralds

# of Lines: 11

Probable Timing: 0.40 minutes

Take Note: Blanche's extraordinarily painful dilemma is underscored by F's orthography, especially it's major punctuation.

Blanche

1   The sun's o'ercast with blood : fair day, adieu !

2   Which is the side that I must go withal ?

3   I am with both, each army hath a hand,
    And in their rage, I having hold of both,
    They whirl [asunder] and dismember me .

4   Husband, I cannot pray that thou mayst win ;
    Uncle, I needs must pray that thou mayst lose ;
    Father, I may not wish the fortune thine ;
    Grandam, I will not wish thy wishes thrive :
    Who ° ever wins, on that side shall I lose ;
    Assured loss before the match be play'd .

Blanche

1　The Sun's orecast with bloud : faire day adieu,
　　Which is the side that I must goe withall?

2　I am with both, each Army hath a hand,
　　And in their rage, I having hold of both,
　　They whurle [a-sunder], and dismember mee .

3　Husband, I cannot pray that thou maist winne :
　　Uncle, I needs must pray that thou maist lose :
　　Father, I may not wish the fortune thine :
　　Grandam, I will not wish thy wishes thrive :
　　Who-ever wins, on that side shall I lose :
　　Assured losse, before the match be plaid .

- her overall nightmare is spelled out with her very first words, the surround phrase ' . The Sun's orecast with bloud : '

- that it is causing her problems can be seen in the ungrammatical nature of F #1, where the adding of the second line to the first via a fast-link comma suggests that she is almost too stunned to know what to do—and certainly F #1 is her most emotional sentence to date (1/4)

- despite the relative calm opening F #2, the extra breath-thought in the last line seems to separate, and thus double, the pain she is undergoing

- F #3 is simply an orthographic extension of the maelstrom she refers to in F #2, for the hammer-blow of five successive logical colons that turn the whole sentence into surround phrases suggests a brainstorm of smothering and contrasting realisations from which she may not escape

The Life and Death of King John

Constance

No, I defie all Counsell, all redresse,
3.4.23–36

Background: despite the marriage of Blanche and the Dolphin, thanks to the papal intervention (see background to and speeches above), war has renewed between English King John on the one side, and France and Austria on the other, with devastating consequences for the latter. The French and Austrian forces have been soundly defeated, Austria is dead, and Constance's son Arthur has been taken prisoner and is on his way to London. Constance, prophetically as it turns out, believes she will never see her son again, and in her grief she makes no attempt to hide her true feelings, so much so that the King of France has just described her as 'a grave unto a soule/Holding th'eternall spirit against her will,/In the vilde prison of afflicted breath'. This speech is triggered by France's 'Patience good Lady, comfort gentle Constance'

Style: each as part of a four handed scene, perhaps in front of a small group of onlookers

Where: the French encampment outside Angiers

To Whom: Philip of France and Pandulph, in front of the Dolphin and perhaps some attendants

# of Lines: 14

Probable Timing: 0.45 minutes

Constance

1　No, I defy all counsel , all redress ,
　　But that which ends all counsel , true redress :
　　Death, death .

2　　　　　　　　　　O amiable, lovely death !

3　Thou odoriferous stench ! sound rottenness !

4　Arise forth from the couch of lasting night,
　　Thou hate and terror to prosperity ,
　　And I will kiss thy detestable bones,
　　And put my eye°balls in thy vaulty brows ,
　　And ring these fingers with thy household worms ,
　　And stop this gap of breath with fulsome dust,
　　And be a carrion monster like thyself .

5　Come, grin on me, and I will think thou smil'st,
　　And buss thee as thy wife .

6　　　　　　　　　　Misery's love,
　　O, come to me !

Constance

1   No, I defie all Counsell, all redresse,
    But that which ends all counsell, true Redresse:
    Death, death, O amiable, lovely death,
    Thou odoriferous stench : sound rottennesse,
    Arise forth from the couch of lasting night,
    Thou hate and terror to prosperitie,
    And I will kisse thy detestable bones,
    And put my eye-balls in thy vaultie browes,
    And ring these fingers with thy houshold wormes,
    And stop this gap of breath with fulsome dust,
    And be a Carrion Monster like thy selfe ;
    Come, grin on me, and I will thinke thou smil'st,
    And busse thee as thy wife : Miseries Love,
    O come to me .

Take Note: F suggests that Constance is being very brusque with the men who have hurt her, and very careful in her appeal for remedy from a surprising source. With its one sentence F also suggests Constance is incredibly focused, whereas most modern texts destroy this by splitting the F text into six separate sentences.

· her dismissal of the French King is essentially emotional (2/4, F's first two lines)

· the surround phrases show where Constance's thoughts are focused: first the appeal to Death as if it were in the room with her

> " : Death, death, O amiable, lovely death, /Thou odoriferous stench : "

and then the conclusion of what has already been a series of sensual and sexual imagery

> " ; Come, grin on me, and I will thinke thou smil'st,/And busse thee as thy wife : Miseries Love,/O come to me . "

· the depth of her need can be seen in that the moment of begging death to 'Arise' and come and she will 'embrace' him (the long seven and a half line section between the second colon and next semicolon), is carefully spoken, as if she doesn't want to frighten him away (2/5, with three of the lines being non-embellished)

· and then as she utters the final surround phrase appeal, spiced with the bribery of promising to kiss Death 'as thy wife' so passion flares (2/2), with emotion on the verbs and intellect on how she sees death, 'Miseries Love'

The Life and Death of King John
Constance

Thou art holy to belye me so,
3.4.44–60

Background: Following on the previous speech, this speech is triggered by the papal legate Pandulph's remonstration 'Lady, you utter madness, and not sorrow'

Style: each as part of a four handed scene, perhaps in front of a small group of onlookers

Where: the French encampment outside Angiers

To Whom: Philip of France and Pandulph, in front of the Dolphin and perhaps some attendants

# of Lines: 17

Probable Timing: 0.55 minutes

Take Note: F's onrushed three sentences reveal far more about Constance's inability to control her thoughts than does the modern text's resetting the speech as seven sentences.

Constance

1   Thou art [not] holy to belie me so,
    I am not mad .

2   This hair I tear is mine,
    My name is Constance, I was Geffrey's wife,
    Young Arthur is my son , and he is lost .

3   I am not mad, I would to heaven I were !
    For then 'tis like I should forget myself .

4   O, if I could, what grief should I forget !

5   Preach some philosophy to make me mad,
    And thou shalt be canoniz'd, Cardinal ;
    For, being not mad, but sensible of grief ,
    My reasonable part produces reason
    How I may be deliver'd of these woes,
    And teaches me to kill or hang myself .

6   If I were mad, I should forget my son ,
    Or madly think a babe of clouts were he .

7   I am not mad ; too well, too well I feel
    The different plague of each calamity .

Constance

1   Thou art [ ] holy to belye me so,
    I am not mad : this haire I teare is mine,
    My name is Constance, I was Geffreyes wife,
    Yong Arthur is my sonne, and he is lost :
    I am not mad, I would to heaven I were,
    For then 'tis like I should forget my selfe :
    O, if I could, what griefe should I forget?

2   Preach some Philosophy to make me mad,
    And thou shalt be Canoniz'd (Cardinall .)

3   For, being not mad, but sensible of greefe,
    My reasonable part produces reason
    How I may be deliver'd of these woes,
    And teaches mee to kill or hang my selfe :
    If I were mad, I should forget my sonne,
    Or madly thinke a babe of clowts were he :
    I am not mad : too well, too well I feele
    The different plague of each calamitie .

- that the speech is emotional rather than intellectual (6/14) is only to be expected, but where the extra spellings often fall (at the end of phrase or line) suggests an unusual pattern of vocal release, as if each idea almost runs away with her, and there are three clusters, 'this haire I teare is mine', and 'teaches mee to kill or hang my selfe', and 'Or madly thinke a babe of clowts were he', where the spoken pain is almost tangible

- the large number of colons (6) is also surprising for such an emotional speech, suggesting that though her feelings are freely flowing, she is still trying to explain and define herself so that the men will understand her and treat her as sane

- that the one phrase repeated several times through out the speech should finally become the only surround phrase in the speech (' : I am not mad : ') hammers home that this is the very spine of all that she is attempting to prove

- there is a fascinating see-saw between passages of energy followed by moments of non-embellished calm (the first phrase line 2; line 5; and the first half of line 6 F #1; plus lines 2, 3, 5, and the first phrase of line 7 and line 8 F #3)

- there are two moments where intellect come into and play momentarily brings her back into the 'real' world—the passionate two and half line passage between the first two F #1 colons when she attempts to define herself through her husband and son (3/4), and F #2's two line attack on Pandulph, the architect of her downfall (3/1)

The Life and Death of King Richard the Second
Queen/Queene

What sport shall we devise here in this Garden,
between 3.4.1–28

Background: knowledge of Richard's capture has spread, though as yet his wife has no clear news. While safe under the protection of the Duke of Yorke, she nevertheless cannot respond to either her own or her women's attempts to raise her spirits.

Style: as part of a three-handed scene

Where: in the garden of the Duke of Yorke's home at Langley

To Whom: her two Ladies

# of Lines: 24

Probable Timing: 1.15 minutes

Take Note: Perhaps taking Bushy's advice to 'lay aside selfe-harming heavinesse', F's orthography shows the Queene's attempts, and especially failures, to successfully follow his counsel.

Queen

1   What sport shall we devise here in this garden
     To drive away the heavy thought of care ?

2   {Bowls ? }

3   Twill make me think the world is full of rubs,
     And that my fortune runs against the bias .

4   My legs can keep no measure in delight,
     When my poor heart no measure keeps in grief ;
     Therefore no dancing, girl , some other sport .

5   {And neither } tales of sorrow, or of grief {,}

     For if of joy, being altogether wanting,
     It doth remember me the more of sorrow ;
     Or if of grief , being altogether had,
     It adds more sorrow to my want of joy ;
     For what I have, I need not to repeat,
     And what I want, it boots not to complain .

6   {If you} sing 'tis well that thou hast cause,
     But thou shouldst please me better wouldst thou weep .

7   And I could sing, would weeping do me good,
     And never borrow any tear of thee .

           Enter a Gardiner, and two Servants

8   But stay, here [come] the gardeners
     Let's step into the shadow of these trees .

9   My wretchedness , unto a row of pins ,
     [They will] talk of state, for every one doth so
     Against a change ; woe is fore°run with woe .

Queene

1 What sport shall we devise here in this Garden,
   To drive away the heavie thought of Care ?

---

2 {Bowles ? }

3 Twill make me thinke the World is full of Rubs,
   And that my fortune runnes against the Byas .

---

4 My Legges can keepe no measure in Delight,
   When my poore Heart no measure keepes in Griefe .

5 Therefore no Dancing (Girle) some other sport .

6 {And neyther}Tales of Sorrow, or of Griefe {,}

For if of Joy, being altogether wanting,
It doth remember me the more of Sorrow :
Or if of Griefe, being altogether had,
It addes more Sorrow to my want of Joy :
For what I have, I need not to repeat ;
And what I want, it bootes not to complaine .

---

7 {If you} sing 'tis well that thou hast cause :
   But thou should'st please me better, would'st thou weepe .

---

8 And I could sing, would weeping doe me good,
   And never borrow any Teare of thee .

Enter a Gardiner, and two Servants

9 But stay, here [comes] the Gardiners,
   Let's step into the shadow of these Trees .

10 My wretchednesse, unto a Rowe of Pinnes,
   [They'le] talke of State : for every one doth so,
   Against a Change ;Woe is fore-runne with Woe .

- the surround phrases clearly show from where her deep sorrow stems, for while the first may seem somewhat oblique

    " : For what I have, I need not to repeat ; "

    those densely packing the last sentence explain what she has been undergoing

    " . My wretchednesse, unto a Rowe of Pinnes,/They'le talke of
        State : for every one doth so,/Against a Change ; Woe is fore-
        runne with Woe . "

- though passion seems to be the hallmark of the speech (28/23 in twenty-four lines overall), it often seems to be more a matter of intellect recognizing an idea only for the following emotional response to negate it, there are moments where she can keep her grief and ennui in check, as with…

- …the opening, where she wants to rid herself of 'Care' (2/0, F #1)

- and in lines 2-5 of F #6, as she herself recognises the paradox that any memory of 'Joy' will only lead her back to 'Sorrow' (5/2)

- and as the 'Gardiners' appear (F #9, 2/0)

- there are two occasions when passion seems to get the better of her,

    a. as she dismisses all forms of entertainment that cross her mind (12/12 in the six and a half lines of F #2 to the first line of F #6)

    b. and the even more concentrated release at the end of the speech at the inevitability of hearing commoners talk of matters of 'State' presumably involving Richard and perhaps herself, (6/7 in just three lines of F #10)

The Life and Death of King Richard the Second

Queen/Queene

Oh I am prest to death through want of speaking :
between 3.4.1–101

Background: having listened to the absent Richard being taken to task by the Gardiners for not taking good care of his 'garden', unobserved and in silence, the Queene is forced to reveal herself and respond.

Style: one on one one address in front of a small group of listeners

Where: in the garden of the Duke of Yorke's home at Langley

To Whom: to the Gardiner, in front of his two servants and her two Ladies

# of Lines: 19

Probable Timing: 1.00 minutes

Take Note: That the impact of the news of Richard's capture and inevitability of his being deposed drives the Queene to a new state of being can be seen in the amazing directness of her phrasing and images (notably in the two short sentences, and even more so in the three surround phrases that start the speech), especially when compared to her previous speeches.

Queen

1   O , I am press'd to death through want of speaking !

2   Thou old Adam's likeness , set to dress this garden,
    How dares thy harsh rude tongue sound this unpleasing
                                                    news ?

3   What Eve, what serpent, hath suggested thee
    To make a second fall of cursed man ?

4   Why dost thou say King Richard is depos'd ?

5   Dar'st thou, thou little better thing [than] earth,
    Divine his downfall ?

6   Say, where, when, and how,
    Cam'st thou by this ill-tidings ?

7   Speak , thou wretch .

---

8   Nimble mischance, that art so light of foot ,
    Doth not thy embassage belong to me,
    And am I last that knows it ?

9   O , thou think'st
    To serve me last, that I may longest keep
    Thy sorrow in my breast .

11   Come, ladies, go ,
    To meet at London London's king in woe .

12 What, was I born to this, that my sad look
    Should grace the triumph of great Bullingbrook ?

13 Gard'ner, for telling me [these] news of woe,
    [Pray God] the plants thou graft'st may never grow .

Queene

1   Oh I am prest to death through want of speaking :
Thou old Adams likenesse, set to dresse this Garden :
How dares thy harsh rude tongue sound this unpleasing
                                                    newes
What Eve ? what Serpent hath suggested thee,
To make a second fall of cursed man ?

2   Why do'st thou say, King Richard is depos'd,
Dar'st thou, thou little better thing [then] earth,
Divine his downfall ?

3   Say, where, when, and how
Cam'st thou by this ill-tydings ?

4   Speake thou wretch .

___

5   Nimble mischance, that art so light of foote,
Doth not thy Embassage belong to me ?

6   And am I last that knowes it ?

7   Oh thou think'st
To serve me last, that I may longest keepe
Thy sorrow in my breast .

8   Come Ladies goe,
To meet at London, Londons King in woe .

9   What was I borne to this : that my sad looke,
Should grace the Triumph of great Bullingbrooke .

10 Gard'ner, for telling me [this] newes of woe,
[I would] the Plants thou graft'st, may never grow .

- that she has no time for courtesy can be seen in the short sentences F #4, 'Speake thou wretch.' and F #6, 'And am I the last that knows it?'

- that the news comes as a hammer blow to her can be seen in the surround phrases opening the speech

  " . Oh I am prest to death through want of speaking : /Thou old
  Adams likenesse, set to dresse this Garden : / How dares thy
  harsh rude tongue sound this unpleasing newes/What Eve ? "

  especially the last, accentuated as it is by the ungrammatical linking of the end of one line 'newes' to the start of the next 'What Eve?' without punctuation (viz. 'newes/What Eve?'), a setting modern texts alter by often starting a new sentence with 'What Eve', thus removing F's suggestion of the Queene's rhetorical distress at this point

- the shock seems to have created a new form of expression within her, for it now seems excesses are not often released (for the 'excess' count here is 13/14 in nineteen lines), and thus the small passage of non-embellished lines speaks volumes as to her new centeredness

  "Dar'st thou, thou little better thing then earth,/Divine his
  downfall? Say, where, when, and how /Cam'st thou by this... "

- however, there is one moment of taking intellectual control (F #8) when her release underscores that she will let nothing stand in her way (4/1 in one and a half lines)

The Life and Death of King Richard the Second

Queene

But soft, but see, or rather doe not see,
between 5.1.7–34

Background: Richard is being conveyed to the Tower. On the way he
is joined by his wife who, despite the dangers, has journeyed from
the safety of the Duke of Yorke's home at Langley (where she has
been under Yorke's protection) to see him. In urging her to flee to
France for her own safekeeping, Richard has stoically accepted his
fate ('I am sworne Brother (Sweet)/To grim Necessitie; and he and
I/Will keep a League till Death'), which pleases her not one bit.

Style: one on one address in front of a small group

Where: public street on the way to the Tower

To Whom: her deposed husband Richard, in front of her Ladies and
his guard

# of Lines: 18

Probable Timing: 0.55 minutes

Take Note: F shows the Queene fighting through her opening emotional shock to use her intellect to try and help Richard: as such,
she displays inner strength without becoming the shrew that often
happens in many modern productions, though her recent tendency
to tears and can be seen at the top of this speech too.

Queen

1   But soft, but see, or rather do not see,
    My faire rose wither ;yet look up, behold,
    That you in pity may dissolve to dew
    And wash him fresh again with true-love tears .

2   Ah, thou, the model where old Troy did stand,
    Thou map of honor, thou King Richard's tomb ,
    And not King Richard ;thou most beauteous inn ,
    Why should hard-favor'd grief be lodg'd in thee,
    When triumph is become an ale°house guest ?

---

3   What, is my Richard both in shape and mind
    Transform'd and weaken'd ?

4   Hath Bullingbrook
    Depos'd thine intellect ?

5   Hath he been in thy heart ?

6   The lion dying thrusteth forth his paw,
    And wounds the earth, if nothing else, with rage
    To be o'er-powr'd, and wilt thou, pupil -like,
    Take thy correction, mildly kiss the rod ,
    And fawn on rage with base humility ,
    Which art a lion and [the] king of beasts ?

Queene

1 But soft, but see, or rather doe not see,
   My faire Rose wither : yet looke up ; behold,
   That you in pittie may dissolve to dew,
   And wash him fresh againe with true-love Teares .

2 Ah thou, the Modell where old Troy did stand,
   Thou Mappe of Honor, thou King Richards Tombe,
   And not King Richard : thou most beauteous Inne,
   Why should hard-favor'd Griefe be lodg'd in thee,
   When Triumph is become an Ale-house Guest .

3 What, is my Richard both in shape and minde
   Transform'd, and weaken'd ?

4   Hath Bullingbrooke
   Depos'd thine Intellect ? hath he beene in thy Heart ?

5 The Lyon dying, thrusteth forth his Paw,
   And wounds the Earth, if nothing else, with rage
   To be o're-powr'd : and wilt thou, Pupill-like,
   Take thy Correction mildly, kisse the Rodde,
   And fawne on Rage with base Humilitie,
   Which art a Lyon, and [a] King of Beasts ?

• her strength can be seen in two tiny orthographical moments: first the surround phrase command to herself and her women not to avoid their eyes at the sight of Richard as a prisoner, ' : yet looke up ; ', and then the onrush of sentence F #4, split in two by most modern texts, demanding an answer from Richard as to whether Bullingbrooke has destroyed his 'Intellect' and 'Heart'

• that the first sight of Richard may be a shock to her can be seen in the contrary instructions in the first two lines of F #1 and the shift in orthography that she opens with, passion in the first line and a half (1/1), and then emotion (1/4) as she expresses a metaphorical image in the hope she and her women can renew him afresh

• the irony and anger of her classical-analogy questioning, demanding why 'Triumph' should reign in the common man while her husband is full of 'Griefe' is ferociously intellectual (14/5 in the five lines of F#2)

• and once she comes face to face with Richard, so she tries to make full use of her intellect to get him to stand up for himself—but as she does so her emotions increase too (15/9 in the nine lines of F #3-5), and at times, especially in the images of strength needed versus the weakness that Richard is currently showing, so four extra breath-thoughts add weight to her argument (see for example the end of F #3 and #5)

The First Part of King Henry the Fourth
Lady Percy/Lady

O my good Lord, why are you thus alone ?
2.3.37–64

Background: Kate, in her first speech in the play, attempts to get her husband Hotspurre to tell her what is disturbing him, knowing that for some time his sleep has been badly interrupted by military dreams.

Style: part of a two-handed scene

Where: Hotspurre's home

To Whom: her husband Hotspurre

# of Lines: 28

Probable Timing: 1.25 minutes

Take Note: With all the passion in the speech, amazingly by the end Kate manages to calm herself down for the final demand to be told what all Hotspurre's recent sleep-talk and unusual behaviour means—a perfect example of staying calm so he must answer, for if she became hysterical he could divert the questioning by asking her to calm herself.

Lady

1　O my good lord, why are you thus alone ?

2　For what offense have I this fortnight been
　A banish'd woman from my Harry's bed ?

3　Tell me, sweet lord, what is't that takes from thee
　Thy stomach , pleasure, and thy golden sleep ?

4　Why dost thou bend thine eyes upon the earth,
　And start so often when thou sit'st alone ?

5　Why hast thou lost the fresh blood in thy cheeks ,
　And given my treasures and my rights of thee
　To thick -ey'd musing and curst melancholy ?

6　In [thy] faint-slumbers I by thee have watch'd,
　And heard thee murmur tales of iron wars ,
　Speak terms of manage to thy bounding steed,
　Cry "Courage! to the field !"

7　　　　　　　　　　　　　　　　And thou hast talk'd
　Of sallies, and retires ; trenches, tents,
　Of palisadoes , frontiers, parapets,
　Of basilisks , of canon, culverin,
　Of prisoners' ransom , and of soldiers slain ,
　And all the [currents] of a heady fight ;
　Thy spirit within thee hath been so at war ,
　And thus hath so bestirr'd thee in thy sleep ,
　That [beads] of sweat [have] stood upon thy brow,
　Like bubbles in a late-disturbed stream ,
　And in thy face strange motions have appear'd,
　Such as we see when men restrain their breath
　On some great sudden [hest] .

8　　　　　　　　　　　　　　　　O, what portents are these ?

9　Some heavy business hath my lord in hand,
　And I must know it, else he loves me not .

Lady

1   O my good Lord, why are you thus alone ?

2   For what offence have I this fortnight bin
     A banish'd woman from my Harries bed ?

3   Tell me (sweet Lord) what is't that takes from thee
     Thy stomacke, pleasure, and thy golden sleepe ?

4   Why dost thou bend thine eyes upon the earth ?
     And start so often when thou sitt'st alone ?

5   Why hast thou lost the fresh blood in thy cheekes ?
     And given my Treasures and my rights of thee,
     To thicke-ey'd musing, and curst melancholly ?

6   In [my] faint-slumbers, I by thee have watcht,
     And heard thee murmore tales of Iron Warres :
     Speake tearmes of manage to thy bounding Steed,
     Cry courage to the field .

7   And thou hast talk'd
     Of Sallies, and Retires ; Trenches, Tents,
     Of Palizadoes, Frontiers, Parapets,
     Of Basiliskes, of Canon, Culverin,
     Of Prisoners ransome, and of Souldiers slaine,
     And all the [current] of a headdy fight .

8   Thy spirit within thee hath beene so at Warre,
     And thus hath so bestirr'd thee in thy sleepe,
     That [beds] of sweate [hath] stood upon thy Brow,
     Like bubbles in a late-disturbed Streame ;
     And in thy face strange motions have appear'd,
     Such as we see when men restraine their breath
     On some great sodaine [hast] .

9   O what portents are these ?

10 Some heavie businesse hath my Lord in hand,
     And I must know it : else he loves me not .

- that the start is tricky for her can be seen in the opening short sentence, and the gradual build through the first six sentences, which moves from pure intellect in asking why she has been 'banish'd' from his bed (2/0, F #1-2), through emotion as she lists his strange behaviours of late (2/6, F #3-5), into passion as she tells him she has heard him talking in his sleep (3/4, F #6)

- she then becomes far more rational than modern texts allow: F #7 merely sums all the individual military terms he has spoken, which then allows her, via F #8, to cap the pressure built argument by showing him that all he has said are signs of a soul deeply disturbed: as such the argument is made far more powerful by being set as two separate sentences rather than being piggybacked onto mt. #7 as in modern texts, that, in combining F #7-8, tend to pass over F's rationality in favour of an almost hysterical finish

- not only does F separate F #7 and #8, it's orthography shows their make-up to be very different

  a. the list of military terms Kate quotes back at Hotspurre is highly intellectual, as if she has memorized everything very carefully (10/2 in the first three and a half lines of F #7)

  b. in summing up the inevitable and dangerous 'headdy fight', thus leading into the 'disturbed soul' sequence, she becomes strongly emotional (5/11 the last two lines of F #7 and all F #8)

- as discussed in the opening comment, F #9-10) are almost non-embellished (1/1 in two and a half lines), as if to ensure that she will be answered rather than fobbed off with emotion, teasing, or an inconsequential reply

The First Part of King Henry the Fourth
Lady Percy/Lady

Out you mad-headed Ape, a Weazell hath not
between 2.3.77–99

Background: instead of answering her Hotspurre has called for his
horse. To her demand of 'What is it carries you away?' Hotspurre
has flippantly replied 'Why, my horse (my Love) my horse', which
triggers the following.

Style: part of a two-handed scene

Where: Hotspurre's home

To Whom: her husband Hotspurre

# of Lines: 12

Probable Timing: 0.40 minutes

Take Note: The shaded area shows where F has started the speech
in more everyday prose (perhaps suggesting that something has
caused her to momentarily relax the tension seen in the previous
speech, and then moves into more vulnerable verse—a switch
doubly weighted by the amazing series of six short sentences (five
monosyllabic) that end the speech. Most modern texts set the
whole speech as verse, removing the contrast between this and the
previous speech, as well as the huge change within this speech between F #5 and F #6-11.

Lady Percy

1   Out, you mad-headed ape !
     A weasel hath not such a deal of spleen
     As you are toss'd with.

2   In [faith],
     I'll know your business , Harry, that I will .

3   I fear my brother Mortimer doth stir
     About his title, and hath sent for you
     To line his enterprise .

4   Come, come, you paraquito, answer me
     Directly unto this question that I [ ] ask .

5   [In faith], I'll break thy little finger, Harry,
     [And] if thou wilt not tell me [all things] true .

6   Do [you] not love me ? do [you] not indeed ?

7   Well, do not then, for since you love me not,
     I will not love myself .

8   Do you not love me ?

9   Nay, tell me if [you speak] in jest or no .

Lady

1   Out you mad-headed Ape, a Weazell hath not
     such a deale of Spleene, as you are tost with .

2   In [sooth] Ile
     know your businesse Harry, that I will .

3   I feare my Bro-
     ther Mortimer doth stirreabout his Title, and hath sent
     for you to line his enterprize .

---

4   Come, come, you Paraquito, answer medirectly
     unto this question, that I [shall] aske .

5   [Indeede], Ile breake
     thy little finger Harry, [ ] if thou wilt not tel me [ ] true .

---

6   Do [ye] not love me ?

7   Do [ye] not indeed ?

8   Well, do not then .

9   For since you love me not,
     I will not love my selfe .

10   Do you not love me ?

11   Nay, tell me if [thou speak'st] in jest, or no .

- while the opening five sentences match, F sets up the start of the verse switch demand 'Do ye not love me?' as four short sentences (F #6-9), with each, because of their shortness, having an expectation of impact or response, a fine debating and rhetorical attack: most modern texts join F #6 with #7, and #8 with #9, thus reducing the rhetorical demand and running the risk of turning the questioning moment into something too rushed and therefore more emotional

- the fact that the short questions are not emotionally spoken, but very carefully posed, can be seen in that while F's prose opening is quite passionate (9/10 in the seven and a half lines F #1-5), the final verse section is not only monosyllabic (save for the one word 'indeed') and composed of nothing but short sentences, and save for the one word 'selfe' non-embellished too

The Second Part of King Henry the Fourth

Hostesse

Oh my most worshipfull Lord, and't please your
between 2.1.69–103

Background: in one of the many financial disputes with Falstaffe, the Hostesse (often known as Mistris Quickly) of the tavern where he lives has brought an action against him, employing two officers, Fang and Snare who have attempted to arrest Falstaffe, with the inevitable result of a street brawl about to erupt. Falstaffe is demanding that Bardolfe 'Cut me off the Villaines head' and Fang and the Hostesse are calling for a 'rescu'. Into the fracas comes Falstaffe's nemesis, the Lord Chiefe Justice, who demands that all concerned 'Keepe the Peace here, hoa'. The following is the Hostesse's attempt to justify her part in the action.

Style: to two people in front of a small group

Where: a London street

To Whom: the Lord Chiefe Justice and Falstaffe, in front of Bardolfe and the officers Fang and Snare

# of Lines: 23

Probable Timing: 1.10 minutes

Take Note: It seems that much of the Falstaffe-Hostesse relationship is to around food, for that's the topic so many of her complaining surround phrases seem to enhance.

Hostesse

1   O my most worshipful lord, and't please your
Grace, I am a poor widow of Eastcheap, and he is arre-
sted at my suit .

---

2   He hath eaten me out of house and home, he hath
put all my substance into that fat belly of his, but I will
have some of it out again , or I will ride thee [a]' nights
like the mare .

---

3   Thou didst swear to me upon a parcel—gilt goblet,
sitting in my Dolphin chamber, at the round table
by a sea-coal fire, [upon] Wednesday in Wheeson week,
when the Prince broke thy head for [liking] him to a sin-
ging man of Windsor, thou didst swear to me then, as I
was washing thy wound, to marry me and make me my
lady thy wife .

4   Canst [thou] deny it ?

5   Did not goodwife Keech, the
butcher's wife, come in then and call me gossip Quickly ?
coming in to borrow a mess of vinegar, telling us she
had a good dish of prawns : whereby [thou] didst desire to
eat some, whereby I told thee they were ill for a green
wound ?

6   And didst [thou not], when she was gone down stairs ,
desire me to be no more [familiarity] with such poor
people, saying, that ere long they should call me madam ?

7   And didst [thou] not kiss me, and bid me fetch thee
[thirty shillings] ?

8   I put thee now to thy book-oath .

9   Deny it if thou canst .

Hostesse

1 Oh my most worshipfull Lord, and't please your
Grace, I am a poore widdow of Eastcheap, and he is arre-
sted at my suit .

2 {†} {H}e hath eaten me out of house and home ; hee hath
put all my substance into that fat belly of his : but I will
have some of it out againe, or I will ride thee [o]'Nights,
like the Mare .

Thou didst sweare to mee upon a parcell gilt Goblet,
sitting in my Dolphin-chamber at the round table,
by a sea-cole fire, [on] Wednesday in Wheeson week,
when the Prince broke thy head for [lik'ning] him to a sin-
ging man of Windsor ; Thou didst sweare to me then (as I
was washing thy wound) to marry me, and make mee my
Lady thy wife .

4 Canst [ÿ] deny it ?

5 Did not goodwife Keech the
Butchers wife come in then, and cal me gossip Quickly ?
comming in to borrow a messe of Vinegar : telling us, she
had a good dish of prawnes : whereby [ÿ] didst desire to
eat some : whereby I told thee they were ill for a greene
wound ?

6 And didst [not thou] (when she was gone downe staires)
desire me to be no more [familiar] with such poore
people, saying, that ere long they should call me Madam ?

7 And didst [ÿ] not kisse me, and bid mee fetch thee [30 .s] ?

8 I
put thee now to thy Book-oath , deny it if thou canst ?

- " . {H}e hath eaten me out of house and home ; hee hath put all my substance into that fat belly of his :"

    " : telling us, she had a good dish of prawnes : whereby ÿ didst desire to eat some : whereby I told thee they were ill for a greene wound ? "

- the self-introduction to the Justice is passionate(3/4, F #1)

- while the beginning of the complaint against Falstaffe opens with an unembellished surround phrase, in part composed by the (emotional) semicolon (as if she were trying to hold herself back?), the food accusation quickly moves into passion again (2/2, F #2)

- as she addresses Falstaffe directly, emotion breaks out on the first line (1/3, first line of F #3) as she accuses him of taking an oath (as she explains at the end of the sentence, to marry her); then, in recalling the facts to pinpoint when and where she turns intellectual (5/1, the next three and a half lines of F #3 to the next semicolon); and, via the new (emotional) semicolon finishes passionately (as Falstaffe's promise to marry her is voiced for all to hear, 2/2)

- the invitation for him to deny this is triply weighted, being a very short, monosyllabic, unembellished sentence

- the naming of a potential witness becomes intellectual once more (4/0, the first two lines of F #5), but then the energy begins to sag, the surround phrases initially doing most of the work as she talks about food once more (0/2, the end of F #5)

- and it seems that she has no idea as to how to continue (perhaps having expected an answer from Falstaffe before now), for while more details about 'goodwife Keech' (the witness) are emotional (1/3, F #6), the last two short sentences, suggesting that she cannot elaborate any more, are first passionate (0/2, F #7, about the kiss, and the money!), and then intellectual (1/0, F#8, asking him once more to deny it)

The Second Part of King Henry the Fourth
Doll Tearsheet/Dol

Charge me ? I scorne you (scurvie Companion)
between 2.4.123–150

Background: with Falstaffe about to be 'going to the Warres', the Hostesse has arranged a tryst for him with his favourite whore, Dol Tearsheet. Despite the Hostesse's protests, Pistoll, accompanied by Bardolfe and Falstaffe's Page, has joined Falstaffe and Dol. Dol is as equally vehemently anti-Pistoll as the Hostesse. The following is triggered by Pistoll's clumsy sexist joke directed first towards the Hostesse and then Dol, ending with 'Then to you (Mistris Dorothie) I will charge you'.

Style: one on one in front of and for the benefit of a small group

Where: an Eastcheap tavern

To Whom: Pistoll, in front of Falstaffe, the Hostesse, Bardolfe, Falstaffe's Page, and perhaps the Drawer

# of Lines: 20

Probable Timing: 1.05 minutes

Take Note: In this outspoken attack on Pistoll, the opening onrush suggests it takes Dol some time to gain full rhetorical self-control—yet interestingly, by F #3 this passage (whose start most modern texts regard as highly ungrammatical, turning F's opening five sentences into no fewer than eleven) begins to display an enormous amount of mental self-discipline (15/3 F #3-5). However, F's latter half of the speech, which modern texts set as is, becomes far more passionate (17/19).

Dol

1   Charge me ?

2   I scorn you, scurvy companion .

3   What, you poor , base, rascally, cheating, lack—linen
    mate !

4   Away, you mouldy rogue, away !

5   I am meat for
    your master .

---

6   Away, you cutpurse rascal ! you filthy bung,
    away !

7   By this wine, I'll thrust my knife in your mouldy
    chaps , [and] you play the saucy cuttle with me .

8   Away,
    you bottle- ale rascal ! you basket-hilt stale juggler , you !

9   Since when, I pray you, sir ?

10   [God's light], with two points on
    your shoulder ?

11   Much !

---

12 Captain ?thou abominable damn'd cheater,
    art thou not asham'd to be call'd captain ?

12   [And] captains
    were of my mind , they would truncheon you out for ta-
    king their names upon you before you have earn'd them .

13 You a captain !you slave, for what ? for tearing a poor
    whore's ruff in a bawdy-house ?

14   He a captain !hang
    him, rogue ! he lives upon mouldy stew'd prunes and
    dried cakes .

15   A captain !

16   [God's light,] these villains will make
    the word [as odious as the word "occupy"], therefore
    captains had need look [to't].

Dol

1 Charge me ?

2   I scorne you (scurvie Companion)
what ? you poore, base, rascally, cheating, lacke-Linnen-
Mate : away you mouldie Rogue, away ; I am meat for
your Master .

3 Away you Cut-purse Rascall, you filthy Bung,
away : By this Wine, Ile thrust my Knife in your mouldie
Chappes, [if] you play the sawcie Cuttle with me .

4   Away
you Bottle-Ale Rascall, you Basket-hilt stale Jugler, you .

5 Since when, I pray you, Sir ? [what], with two Points on
your shoulder ?much .

6 Captaine ?thou abhominable damn'd Cheater,
art thou not asham'd to be call'd Captaine ?

7   [If] Captaines
were of my minde, they would trunchion you out, for taking their Names upon you, before you have earn'd them .

8 You a Captaine ? you slave, for what ? for tearing a poore
Whores Ruffe in a Bawdy-house ?

9   Hee a Captaine ? hang
him Rogue, hee lives upon mouldie stew'd-Pruines, and
dry'de Cakes .

10   A Captaine ?

11   [ ] These Villaines will make
the word [Captaine odious]: Therefore Captaines had
neede looke [to it] .

- Dol's contempt for Pistoll smacks through the few surround phrases in the speech

    " : away you mouldie Rogue, away; I am meat for your Master . "

    " . Away you Cut-purse Rascall, you filthy Bung, away : "

    " . These Villaines will make the word captaine odious : Therefore Captaines had neede looke to it . "

- the incredibly withheld, short, monosyllabic, non-embellished opening "Charge me?' is the only moment of self-control in the speech, and gives no sign of the explosion that is to come

- the initial invective, denying Pistoll ('you filthy Bung') any chance with her ('I am meat for your Master') is highly passionate (5/4 in the three lines of F #2), more so in F by being an onrushed sentence (split into three by most modern texts)

- and then her scorn becomes amazingly mentally focused as she tells Pistoll to get 'Away' (15/3 in the five and a half lines of F 3-5), again made more powerful by the onrush of three sentences as opposed to the modern texts' six

- finally, she rips apart Pistoll's pretensions in calling himself a 'Captaine', her emotions join her already established intellectual scorn as she does, (an unrelenting 17/19 in nine and a half lines)

The Life of Henry the Fift

Hostess/Hostesse

Nay sure, hee's not in Hell : hee's in Arthurs bosome

2.3.9–26

Background: at the top of the play and as announced in an earlier scene, Falstaffe, never seen in this play, was very ill, and has died offstage. Now his friends are leaving for the French war, still shaken by his loss. Pistoll, with peace now declared between him and Nym, has attempted to cheer them all up, but Bardolfe, probably the closest of Falstaffe's companions, has commented 'Would I were with him, wheresomere hee is, eyther in Heaven, or in Hell', which triggers the following.

Style: general address as part of a five handed scene

Where: outside an Eastcheap tavern

To Whom: Bardolfe, Pistoll, Nym, and Falstaffe's Boy

# of Lines: 16

Probable Timing: 0.55 minutes

Take Note: Quite fascinatingly, F's orthography suggests that all of Mistresse Quickly's energy is invested in the top of the speech, but as she describes how she advised the dying Falstaffe that he 'should not thinke of God' her energy begins to dissipate until there are no extra releases by the last two and half lines of the speech – perhaps not only the content but also the onrushed nature of the speech has had an impact on her.

Hostess

1   Nay sure, he's not in Hell ; he's in Arthur's
bosom , if ever man went to Arthur's bosom .

2   A made a
finer end, and went away and it had been any christom
child .

3   A parted ev'n just between twelve and one, ev'n
at the turning o'th' tide ; for after I saw him fumble with
the sheets, and play with flowers, and smile upon his finger's end, I knew there was but one way ; for his nose was
as sharp as a pen, and a [babbl'd] of green fields .

4   "How now,
Sir John ?" quoth I, "what, man ? be a good cheer ."

5   So a
cried out, "God, God, God !" three or four times .

6   Now I,
to comfort him, bid him a should not think of God ; I
hop'd there was no need to trouble himself with any
such thoughts yet .

7   So a bad me lay more clothes on his
feet .

8   I put my hand into the bed and felt them, and they
were as cold as any stone ; then I felt to his knees, and so
[up' ard] and up'ard , and all was as cold as any stone .

Hostesse

1 Nay sure, hee's not in Hell : hee's in Arthurs
Bosome, if ever man went to Arthurs Bosome : a made a
finer end, and went away and it had beene any Christome
Child : a parted ev'n just betweene Twelve and One, ev'n
at the turning o'th'Tyde : for after I saw him fumble with
the Sheets, and play with Flowers, and smile upon his fingers end, I knew there was but one way : for his Nose was
as sharpe as a Pen, and a [Table] of greene fields .

2   How now
Sir John (quoth I ?) what man ? be a good cheare : so a
cryed out, God, God, God, three or foure times : now I,
to comfort him, bid him a should not thinke of God ; I
hop'd there was no neede to trouble himselfe with any
such thoughts yet : so a bad me lay more Clothes on his
feet : I put my hand into the Bed, and felt them, and they
were as cold as any stone : then I felt to his knees, and so
[up-peer'd], and upward, and all was as cold as any stone .

- the other surround phrases, found in F #2, all seem to be indelibly etched into her mind, viz. " : now I, to comfort him, bid him a should not thinke of God ; I hop'd there was no neede to trouble himselfe with any such thoughts yet : so a bad me lay more Clothes on his feet : ", though even the beginning of F #2 could be seen to be formed by surround phrases too

- but as she begins to describe his behaviour fumbling 'with the Sheets, so the facts takes over (5/2, the last three and a half lines of F #1)

- while recounting her conversation with him brings out more emotion (6/4 in the first three lines of F #2), though quiet, she becomes less controlled and more emotional recalling his last words and her putting the sheets on him (1/2 the two and half lines of F #2 from the semicolon to the final colon)

- but with the final description of his body being cold excesses all but disappear (0/1), as if the memory has struck her so hard that her reliving/recounting it takes everything out of her

The Life of King Henry the Eight
Old Lady

By {your} troth, and Maidenhead,/{You} would not...
between 2.3.23–49

Background: following Henry's first meeting with Anne Bullen, his
attempts to divorce himself from Katherine have proceeded apace,
to the point that she is about to be publicly arraigned (see speeches
#5-8 above). In a private conversation with her chaperone/Duenna,
Anne, whether disingenuously or no, voices her apparent lack of interest in becoming Queene, which triggers the following.

Style: as part of a two-handed scene

Where: unspecified, presumably somewhere in Anne Bullen's private
chambers

To Whom: Anne Bullen

# of Lines: 24

Probable Timing: 1.15 minutes

Take Note: F's sentence structure reveals a totally different character
than that set by most modern texts. The gossipy and at times flab-
bergasted fast release implied in F is virtually wiped out by most
modern texts syntactical reworking of F's six sentences into twelve.
And F's orthography clearly shows the Old Lady's movement from
intellectual amazement into a final session of passionate advice.

Old Lady {†}

1   By {your} troth and maidenhead,
    {You} would not be a queen .

2   Beshrew me, I would,
    And venture maidenhead for't, and so would you
    For all this spice of your hypocrisy .

3   You, that have so fair parts of woman on you,
    Have, too, a woman's heart, which ever yet
    Affected eminence, wealth, sovereignty ;
    Which, to say sooth, are blessings;and which gifts
    (Saving your mincing) the capacity
    Of your soft [cheveril] conscience would receive,
    If you might please to stretch it .

4   You would not be a queen ?
    {†} for all the riches under heaven .

5   Tis strange .

6   A threepence bow'd would hire me,
    Old as I am, to queen it .

7   But I pray you,
    What think you of a duchess ?

8   {If you have not} limbs
    To bear that load of title

    Then you are weakly made ; pluck off a little,
    I would not be a young count in your way
    For more [than] blushing comes to .

9   If your back
    Cannot vouchsafe this burthen, tis too weak
    Ever to get a boy .

10   In faith, for little England
    You'ld venture an emballing .

11   I myself
    Would for [Carnarvonshire], although there 'long'd
    No more to th' crown but that .

12 Lo, who comes here ?

Old Lady {†}

1 By {your} troth, and Maidenhead,
{You} would not be a Queene .

2   Beshrew me, I would,
And venture Maidenhead for't, and so would you
For all this spice of your Hipocrisie :
You that have so faire parts of Woman on you,
Have (too) a Womans heart, which ever yet
Affected Eminence, Wealth, Soveraignty ;
Which, to say sooth, are Blessings ; and which guifts
(Saving your mincing) the capacity
Of your soft [Chiverell] Conscience, would receive,
If you might please to stretch it .

3   {†}ou would not be a Queen ?
{†} for all the riches under Heaven .

4 Tis strange ; a threepence bow'd would hire me
Old as I am, to Queene it : but I pray you,
What thinke you of a Dutchesse ?

5   {If you have not} limbs
To beare that load of Title

Then you are weakly made ; plucke off a little,
I would not be a young Count in your way,
For more [then] blushing comes to : If your backe
Cannot vouchsafe this burthen, tis too weake
Ever to get a Boy .

6   In faith, for little England
You'ld venture an emballing : I my selfe
Would for [Carnarvanshire], although there long'd
No more to th'Crowne but that:Lo, who comes here ?

- after the passionate first sentence (2/1) F's Old Lady lets loose with a strongly intellectual drive (14/7, F #2-4) as she pulls Anne apart for her 'Hipocrisie' in suggesting she (Anne) 'would not be a Queene'— with a wonderfully earthy joke about advancements being made 'if you might please to stretch it', (supposedly referring to 'your soft Chiverell Conscience', a hardly innocent comparison invoking the soft leather ('Chiverell') of a glove

- indeed, the only two short sentences in the speech go right to the heart of calling Anne's bluff, F #1's,

    "By your troth, and Maidenhead,/You would not be a Queene ."
        and F #3's

    " You would not be a Queen ?/for all the riches under Heaven ."

- the Old Lady's own longing for 'Eminence, Wealth, Soveraignty' might well be underscored by the totally emotional semicolon cre-ated surround phrase that follows this list ' ; Which, to say sooth are Blessings ; '

- and then as the Old lady becomes more frankly sexual in her com-ments and advice, her passions are released (10/9, F #4-6)

- interestingly with the excesses elsewhere, now two sexual-political facts of life are spoken without any embellishment; first, Anne's being unable or unwilling to accept her role in love-making for ad-vancement is dismissed tersely with the extra weighted semicoloned surround phrase ' . Then you are weakly made ; ' because in all frank-ness ' For more than blushing comes to'—presumably winning big rewards

- and the humour becomes even earthier, with the final sentence sur-round phrase comment ' . In faith, for little England/You'ld venture an emballing : '

The Life of King Henry the Eight
Queen/Queene

Ye tell me what ye wish for both, my ruine :
between 3.1.98–124

Background: having failed to gain a divorce in public, the two Cardinals have come to Katherine's private chambers to 'know/ How you stand minded in the waighty difference/between the King and you'. In so doing they suggest they will 'deliver/(Like free and honest men) our just opinions /And comforts to [your] cause'—an argument she rejects completely. This speech focuses in their (lack of) integrity.

Style: ach as part of a three-handed scene, in front of a smaller group

Where: the Queene's personal chambers

To Whom: the Cardinalls Wolsey and Campeius, in front of her attendants

# of Lines: 21

Probable Timing: 1.15 minutes

Queen

1　Ye tell me what ye wish for both—my ruin .

2　Is this your Christian counsel ?

3　　　　　　　　　　　　Out upon ye !

4　Heaven is above all yet ; there sits a judge
　That no king can corrupt .

5　The more shame for ye !

6　　　　　　　　　　Holy men I thought ye,
　Upon my soul , two reverend cardinal virtues;
　But cardinal sins and hollow hearts I fear ye .

7　Mend 'em for shame my lords !

8　　　　　　　　　　　　Is this your comfort ?

9　The cordial that ye bring a wretched lady,
　A woman lost among ye, laugh'd at, scorn'd ?

10　Ye turn me into nothing !

11　　　　　　　　　　Woe upon ye,
　And all such false professors !

12　　　　　　　　　　Would you have me
　(If you have any justice, any pity ,
　If ye be any thing but churchmen's habits)
　Put my sick cause into his hands, that hates me ?

13　Alas, [h'as] banish'd me his bed already,
　His love, too long ago !

14　　　　　　　　　　I am old, my lords,
　And all the fellowship I hold now with him
　Is only my obedience .

15　　　　　　　　　What can happen
　To me above this wretchedness ?

16　　　　　　　　　All your studies
　Make me a curse like this !

Queene

1   Ye tell me what ye wish for both, my ruine :
    Is this your Christian Councell ?

2   Out upon ye .

3   Heaven is above all yet ; there sits a Judge .

4   That no King can corrupt .

5   The more shame for ye ; holy men I thought ye,
    Upon my Soule two reverend Cardinall Vertues :
    But Cardinall Sins, and hollow hearts I feare ye :
    Mend 'em for shame my Lords : Is this your comfort ?

6   The Cordiall that ye bring a wretched Lady ?

7   A woman lost among ye, laugh't at, scornd ?

8   Ye turne me into nothing .

9   Woe upon ye,
    And all such false Professors .

10   Would you have me
    (If you have any Justice, any Pitty,
    If ye be any thing but Churchmens habits)
    Put my sicke cause into his hands, that hates me ?

11 Alas, [ha's] banish'd me his Bed already,
    His Love, too long ago .

12   I am old my Lords,
    And all the Fellowship I hold now with him
    Is onely my Obedience .

13   What can happen
    To me, above this wretchednesse ?

14   All your Studies
    Make me a Curse, like this .

- the fact that the six pieces of major punctuation are only found in the opening (up to F #5) suggest that, despite the two emotional semicolons, initially she is working very hard to ensure that the two adversaries are under no illusion about what she has to say

- the surround phrases express her underlying fear

    " : But Cardinall Sins, and hollow hearts I feare ye : /Mend 'em for shame my Lords : Is this your comfort ? "

- the importance to her of stressing that there is a 'Judge' above them all that 'No King can corrupt.' can be seen in the grammatically appalling yet emotionally and rhetorically understandable period ending F #3 – most modern texts set no punctuation here at all

- yet on occasion she still manages to become very calm, wasting no energy when she wants a point to be clearly understood

    "Ye tell me what ye wish for both,...Out upon ye"

    "The more shame for ye ; holy men I thought ye,"

    "A woman lost among ye, laugh't at, scornd?"

    "Woe upon ye,"

- while the overall speech seems intellectually driven (24/12) , F's orthography suggests that it takes her a time to get to control, for the opening sentence is passionate (2/2), as is the attack on the Cardinals (lines 2-3 of F #5, 5/4)

- and once this attack is finished, she takes intellectual charge of the rest of the speech (15/5 in the last thirteen and a half lines) – no matter how difficult control may be at times (as the short sentences show)

- however, as she finishes, she needs two extra breaths to maintain her composure (F #13-14)

The Life of King Henry the Eight
Queen/Queene

Have I liv'd thus long (let me speake my selfe, . . .
between 3.1.125–142

Background: Following on the previous speech, this speech explains why she is so adamantly determined not to grant Henry a divorce.

Style: part of a three-handed scene, in front of a smaller group

Where: the Queene's personal chambers

To Whom: the Cardinalls Wolsey and Campeius, in front of her attendants

# of Lines: 17

Probable Timing: 0.55 minutes

Take Note: In her losing attempt to fight the Cardinals, Katherine poses some very personal rhetorical questions that the Cardinals cannot answer, and shouldn't be expected to. This is especially seen in the five short questions in the middle of the speech (F #4-8). Similarly, the split-line start of the last sentence also suggests that the first moment as she decides to defy Henry and the Cardinals is quite awkward.

Queen

1   Have I liv'd thus long (let me speak myself,
Since virtue finds no friends) a wife, a true one ?

2   A woman (I dare say without vainglory)
Never yet branded with suspicion ?

3   Have I with all my full affections
Still met the King ? lov'd him next heav'n ? obey'd him ?
Been , out of fondness , superstitious to him ?
Almost forgot my pray'rs to content him ?
And am I thus rewarded ?

4   'Tis not well, lords .

5   Bring me a constant woman to her husband,
One that ne'er dream'd a joy beyond his pleasure ;
And to that woman (when she has done most)
Yet will I add an honor—a great patience .

---

6   My lord, I dare not make myself so guilty
To give up willingly that noble title
Your master wed me to .

7   Nothing but death
Shall e'er divorce my dignities .

Queene

1   Have I liv'd thus long (let me speake my selfe,
     Since Vertue findes no friends) a Wife, a true one ?

2   A Woman (I dare say without Vainglory)
     Never yet branded with Suspition ?

3   Have I, with all my full Affections
     Still met the King ?

4   Lov'd him next Heav'n ?

5   Obey'd him ?

6   Bin (out of fondnesse) superstitious to him ?

7   Almost forgot my Prayres to content him ?

8   And am I thus rewarded ?

9   'Tis not well Lords .

10   Bring me a constant woman to her Husband,
     One that ne're dream'd a Joy, beyond his pleasure ;
     And to that Woman (when she has done most)
     Yet will I adde an Honor ; a great Patience .

---

11   My Lord,
     I dare not make my selfe so guiltie,
     To give up willingly that Noble Title
     Your Master wed me to : nothing but death
     Shall e're divorce my Dignities .

- despite the awkwardness revealed by F's sentence structure, line structures, and occasional surround phrase and non-embellished phrases, Katherine manages to retain her intellectual control (18/3 for nearly all the speech, the fourteen lines F #2-11), suggesting that she will be have a much greater impact on both Cardinals and the audience with her dignified but revealing questions and responses than by falling into unnecessary emotional histrionics

- though having to speak of her 'Vertue' herself, Katherine is not able to contain her emotions at the top of the speech (2/4, F #1)

- the two surround phrases express very clearly her defiance of giving Henry an easy way out of their marriage, pointing out that she possesses ' ; a great Patience . ', and that ' : nothing but death/Shall e're divorce my Dignities . '

- the reason for defiance is very clearly expressed in her characteristic firm non-embellished way, doubly weighted by being set in short sentences "Obey'd him?" (F #5) and "And am I thus rewarded?" (F #8)

The Life of King Henry the Eight
Queen/Queene
Would I had never trod this English Earth,
between 3.1.143–184

Background: Following up on the prior 2 speeches in this speech the overwhelming inevitability of her situation seems to have struck home

Style: each as part of a three-handed scene, in front of a smaller group

Where: the Queene's personal chambers

To Whom: the Cardinalls Wolsey and Campeius, in front of her attendants

# of Lines: 21

Probable Timing: 1.15 minutes

Take Note: Queene Katherine's very strong sense of self-control is seen once more throughout this speech, no matter how much effort it costs her to maintain.

Queen

1 Would I had never trod this English earth,
   Or felt the flatteries that grow upon it !

2 Ye have angels' faces, but heaven knows your hearts .

3 What will become of me now, wretched lady ?

4 I am the most unhappy woman living .

5 Alas, poor wenches, where are now your fortunes ?

6 Shipwrack'd upon a kingdom , where no pity ,
   No friends, no hope, no kindred weep for me,
   Almost no grave allow'd me .

7   Like the lily
   That once was mistress of the field, and flourish'd,
   I'll hang my head and perish .

8 Do what ye will, my lords; and pray forgive me ;
   If I have us'd myself unmannerly,
   You know I am a woman, lacking wit
   To make a seemly answer to such persons .

9 Pray do my service to his Majesty ;
   He has my heart yet and shall have my prayers
   While I shall have my life .

10   Come, reverend fathers,
   Bestow your counsels on me .

11   She now begs
   That little thought, when she set footing here ,
   She should have bought her dignities so dear .

Queene

1   Would I had never trod this English Earth,
    Or felt the Flatteries that grow upon it :
    Ye have Angels Faces; but Heaven knowes your hearts .

2   What will become of me now, wretched Lady ?

3   I am the most unhappy Woman living .

4   Alas (poore Wenches) where are now your Fortunes ?

5   Shipwrack'd upon a Kingdome, where no Pitty,
    No Friends, no Hope, no Kindred weepe for me ?
    Almost no Grave allow'd me ?

6   Like the Lilly
    That once was Mistris of the Field, and flourish'd,
    Ile hang my head, and perish .

---

7   Do what ye will, my Lords :
    And pray forgive me ;
    If I have us'd my selfe unmannerly,
    You know I am a Woman, lacking wit
    To make a seemely answer to such persons .

8   Pray do my service to his Majestie,
    He ha's my heart yet, and shall have my Prayers
    While I shall have my life .

9   Come reverend Fathers,
    Bestow your Councels on me .

10   She now begges
    That little thought when she set footing heere,
    She should have bought her Dignities so deere .

- that her antipathy towards the Cardinals is as strong as ever can be seen in the two surround phrases ending F #1

  " : Ye have Angels Faces ; but Heaven knowes your hearts . "

  and the importance of knowing she must apologise at least for form's sake is expressed via

  " . Do what ye will, My Lords : /And pray forgive me ; "

  both doubly weighted by being formed in part by emotional semicolons

- and though the speech stays strongly intellectual throughout (25/7) until the last sentence, nevertheless the two short sentences in the early part of the speech (F #2, defining herself as 'the most unhappy Woman living' and F #3, taking pity on her women) show that at times there is very little time for extended thinking or rhetorical embellishment

- in addition, the non-embellished lines point to her bleak awareness of her impending status (as to be soon ex-wife and ex-Queen), "Ile hang my head, and perish.' and 'He ha's my heart yet…/While I shall have my life.'

- thus at the end of the speech, after asking advice of the men she has denounced so vehemently throughout as false to her cause, it's not surprising that her reflective moment becomes emotional (1/3, F #10): what is surprising is where the spoken emphasis falls, at the end of each line as if the thought (further enhanced by the rhyming couplet) may be moving her to tears

BIBLIOGRAPHY

AND

APPENDICES

BIBLIOGRAPHY

The most easily accessible general information is to be found under the citations of *Campbell,* and of *Halliday.* The finest summation of matters academic is to be found within the all-encompassing *A Textual Companion,* listed below in the first part of the bibliography under *Wells, Stanley and Taylor, Gary* (eds.)

Individual modem editions consulted are listed below under the separate headings 'The Complete Works in Compendium Format' and 'The Complete Works in Separate Individual Volumes,' from which the modem text audition speeches have been collated and compiled.

All modem act, scene, and/or line numbers refer the reader to *The Riverside Shakespeare,* in my opinion still the best of the complete works, despite the excellent compendiums that have been published since.

The F/Q material is taken from a variety of already published sources, including not only all the texts listed in the 'Photostatted Reproductions in Compendium Format' below, but also earlier individually printed volumes, such as the twentieth century editions published under the collective title *The Facsimiles of Plays from The First Folio of Shakespeare* by Faber & Gwyer, and the nineteenth century editions published on behalf of The New Shakespere Society.

The heading 'Single Volumes of Special Interest' is offered to newcomers to Shakespeare in the hope that the books may add useful knowledge about the background and craft of this most fascinating of theatrical figures.

PHOTOSTATTED REPRODUCTIONS OF THE ORIGINAL TEXTS IN COMPENDIUM FORMAT

Allen, M.J.B. and K. Muir, (eds.). *Shakespeare's Plays in Quarto.* Berkeley: University of California Press, 1981.

Blaney, Peter (ed.). *The Norton Facsimile (The First Folio of Shakespeare).* New York: W.W.Norton & Co., Inc., 1996 (see also Hinman, below).

Brewer D.S. (ed.). *Mr. William Shakespeare's Comedies, Histories & Tragedies, The Second/Third/Fourth Folio Reproduced in Facsimile.* (3 vols.), 1983.

Hinman, Charlton (ed.). *The Norton Facsimile (The First Folio of Shakespeare)*. New York: W.W.Norton & Company, Inc., 1968.

Kokeritz, Helge (ed.). *Mr. William Shakespeare 's Comedies, Histories & Tragedies*. New Haven: Yale University Press, 1954.

Moston, Doug (ed.). *Mr. William Shakespeare's Comedies, Histories, and Tragedies*. New York: Routledge, 1998.

MODERN TYPE VERSION OF THE FIRST FOLIO IN COMPENDIUM FORMAT

Freeman, Neil. (ed.). *The Applause First Folio of Shakespeare in Modern Type*. New York & London: Applause Books, 2001.

MODERN TEXT VERSIONS OF THE COMPLETE WORKS IN COMPENDIUM FORMAT

Craig, H. and D. Bevington (eds.). *The Complete Works of Shakespeare*. Glenview: Scott, Foresman and Company, 1973.

Evans, G.B. (ed.). *The Riverside Shakespeare*. Boston: Houghton Mifflin Company, 1974.

Wells, Stanley and Gary Taylor (eds.). *The Oxford Shakespeare, William Shakespeare , the Complete Works, Original Spelling Edition,* Oxford: The Clarendon Press, 1986.

Wells, Stanley and Gary Taylor (eds.). *The Oxford Shakespeare, William Shakespeare, The Complete Works, Modern Spelling Edition*. Oxford: The Clarendon Press, 1986.

MODERN TEXT VERSIONS OF THE COMPLETE WORKS IN SEPARATE INDIVIDUAL VOLUMES

The Arden Shakespeare. London: Methuen & Co. Ltd., Various dates, editions, and editors .

Folio Texts. Freeman, Neil H. M. (ed.) Applause First Folio Editions, 1997, and following.

The New Cambridge Shakespeare. Cambridge: Cambridge University Press. Various dates, editions, and editors.

New Variorum Editions of Shakespeare. Furness, Horace Howard (original editor.). New York: 1880, Various reprints. All these volumes have been in a state of re-editing and reprinting since they first appeared in 1880. Various dates, editions, and editors.

The Oxford Shakespeare. Wells, Stanley (general editor). Oxford: Oxford University Press, Various dates and editors.

The New Penguin Shakespeare . Harmondsworth, Middlesex: Penguin Books, Various dates and editors.

The Shakespeare Globe Acting Edition. Tucker, Patrick and Holden, Michael. (eds.). London: M.H.Publications, Various dates.

SINGLE VOLUMES OF SPECIAL INTEREST

Baldwin, T.W. *William Shakespeare's Petty School.* 1943.

Baldwin, T.W. *William Shakespeare's Small wtin and Lesse Greeke.* (2 vols.) 1944.

Barton, John. *Playing Shakespeare.* 1984.

Beckerman, Bernard. *Shakespeare at the Globe, I 599-1609.* 1962. Berryman, John. *Berryman 's Shakespeare.* 1999.

Bloom, Harold. *Shakespeare: The Invention of the Human.* 1998. Booth, Stephen (ed.). *Shakespeare's Sonnets.* 1977.

Briggs, Katharine. *An Encyclopedia of Fairies.* 1976.

Campbell, Oscar James, and Edward G. Quinn (eds.). *The Reader's Encyclopedia of Shakespeare.* 1966.

Crystal, David, and Ben Crystal. *Shakespeare's Words: A Glossary & Language Companion.* 2002.

Flatter, Richard. *Shakespeare's Producing Hand.* 1948 (reprint).

Ford, Boris. (ed.). *The Age of Shakespeare.* 1955.

Freeman, Neil H.M. *Shakespeare's First Texts.* 1994.

Greg, W.W. *The Editorial Problem in Shakespeare: A Survey of the Foundations of the Text.* 1954 (3rd. edition).

Gurr, Andrew . *Playgoing in Shakespeare's London.* 1987. Gurr, Andrew. *The Shakespearean Stage, 1574-1642.* 1987. Halliday, F.E. *A Shakespeare Companion.* 1952.

Harbage, Alfred. *Shakespeare's Audience.* 1941.

Harrison, G.B. (ed.). *The Elizabethan Journals.* 1965 (revised, 2 vols.).

Harrison, G.B. (ed.). *A Jacobean Journal.* 1941.

Harrison, G.B. (ed.). *A Second Jacobean Journal.* 1958.

Hinman, Charlton. *The Printing and Proof Reading of the First Folio of Shakespeare.* 1963 (2 vols.).

Joseph, Bertram. *Acting Shakespeare.* 1960.

Joseph, Miriam (Sister). *Shakespeare's Use of The Arts of wnguage.* 1947.

King, T.J. *Casting Shakespeare's Plays.* 1992.

Lee, Sidney and C.T. Onions. *Shakespeare's England : An Account Of The Life And Manners Of His Age.* (2 vols.) 1916.

Linklater, Kristin. *Freeing Shakespeare's Voice.* 1992.

Mahood, M .M. *Shakespeare's Wordplay.* 1957.

O'Connor, Gary. *William Shakespeare: A Popular Life.* 2000.

Ordish, T.F. *Early London Theatres.* 1894. (1971 reprint).

Rodenberg, Patsy. *Speaking Shakespeare.* 2002.

Schoenbaum. S. *William Shakespeare: A Documentary Life.* 1975.

Shapiro, Michael. *Children of the Revels.* 1977.

Simpson, Percy. *Shakespeare's Punctuation.* 1969 (reprint).

Smith, Irwin. *Shakespeare's Blackfriars Playhouse .* 1964.

Southern, Richard. *The Staging of Plays Before Shakespeare.* 1973.

Spevack, M. *A Complete and Systematic Concordance to the Works Of Shakespeare .* 1968-1980 (9vols.).

Tillyard, E.M.W. *The Elizabethan World Picture.* 1942.

Trevelyan, G.M. (ed.). *Illustrated English Social History.* 1942.

Vendler, Helen. *The Art of Shakespeare's Sonnets.* 1999.

Walker, Alice F. *Textual Problems of the First Folio.* 1953.

Walton, J.K. *The Quarto Copy of the First Folio.* 1971.

Warren, Michael. *William Shakespeare, The Parallel King Lear 1608-1623.*

Wells, Stanley and Taylor, Gary (eds.). *Modernising Shakespeare's Spelling, with Three Studies in The Text of Henry V.* 1975.

Wells, Stanley. *Re-Editing Shakespeare for the Modern Reader.* 1984.

Wells, Stanley and Gary Taylor (eds.). *William Shakespeare: A Textual Companion .* 1987.

Wright, George T. *Shakespeare's Metrical Art.* 1988.

HISTORICAL DOCUMENTS

Daniel, Samuel. *The Fowre Bookes of the Civile Warres Between The Howses Of Lancaster and Yorke.* 1595.

Holinshed, Raphael. *Chronicles of England, Scotland and Ireland.* 1587 (2nd. edition).

Halle, Edward. *The Union of the Two Noble and Illustre Famelies of Lancastre And Yorke.* 1548 (2nd. edition).

Henslowe, Philip: Foakes, R.A. and Rickert (eds.). *Henslowe's Diary.* 1961.

Plutarch: North, Sir Thomas (translation of a work in French prepared by Jacques Amyots). *The Lives of The Noble Grecians and Romanes.* 1579.

APPENDIX 1:
GUIDE TO THE EARLY TEXTS

A QUARTO (Q)

A single text, so called because of the book size resulting from a particular method of printing. Eighteen of Shakespeare's plays were published in this format by different publishers at various dates between 1594-1622, prior to the appearance of the 1623 Folio.

THE FIRST FOLIO (F1)'

Thirty-six of Shakespeare's plays (excluding *Pericles* and *Two Noble Kinsmen,* in which he had a hand) appeared in one volume, published in 1623. All books of this size were termed Folios, again because of the sheet size and printing method, hence this volume is referred to as the First Folio. For publishing details see Bibliography, 'Photostated Reproductions of the Original Texts.'

THE SECOND FOLIO (F2)

Scholars suggest that the Second Folio, dated 1632 but perhaps not published until 1640, has little authority, especially since it created hundreds of new problematic readings of its own. Nevertheless more than 800 modern text readings can be attributed to it. The **Third Folio** (1664) and the **Fourth Folio** (1685) have even less authority, and are rarely consulted except in cases of extreme difficulty.

APPENDIX 2:
WORD, WORDS, WORDS

PART ONE: VERBAL CONVENTIONS (AND HOW THEY WILL BE SET
IN THE FOLIO TEXT)

"THEN" AND "THAN"

These two words, though their neutral vowels sound different to modern
ears, were almost identical to Elizabethan speakers and readers, despite
their different meanings. F and Q make little distinction between them,
setting them interchangeably . The original setting will be used, and the
modern reader should soon get used to substituting one for the other as
necessary.

"I," "AY," AND "AYE"

F/Q often print the personal pronoun "I" and the word of agreement
"aye" simply as "I." Again, the modern reader should quickly get used
to this and make the substitution when necess ary. The reader should
also be aware that very occasionally either word could be used and the
phrase make perfect sense, even though different meanings would be
implied.

"MY SELFE/HIM SELFE/HER SELFE" VERSUS "MYSELF/HIMSELF/HER-SELF"

Generally F/Q separate the two parts of the word, "my selfe" while
most modern texts set the single word "myself." The difference is vital,
based on Elizabethan philosophy. Elizabethans regarded themselves
as composed of two parts, the corporeal "I," and the more spiritual
part, the "self." Thus, when an Elizabethan character refers to "my
selfe," he or she is often referring to what is to all intents and purposes
a separate being, even if that being is a particular part of him- or herself. Thus soliloquies can be thought of as a debate between the "I" and
"my selfe," and, in such speeches, even though there may be only one
character on-stage, it's as if there were two distinct entities present.

UNUSUAL SPELLING OF REAL NAMES, BOTH OF PEOPLE AND PLACES

Real names, both of people and places, and foreign languages are often reworked for modern understanding. For example, the French town often set in Fl as "Callice" is usually reset as "Calais." F will be set as is.

NON-GRAMMATICAL USES OF VERBS IN BOTH TENSE AND APPLICATION

Modern texts 'correct' the occasional Elizabethan practice of setting a singular noun with plural verb (and vice versa), as well as the infrequent use of the past tense of a verb to describe a current situation. The F reading will be set as is, without annotation.

ALTERNATIVE SETTINGS OF A WORD WHERE DIFFERENT SPELLINGS MAINTAIN THE SAME MEANING

F/Q occasionally set what appears to modern eyes as an archaic spelling of a word for which there is a more common modern alternative, for example "murther" for murder , "burthen" for burden, "moe" for more, "vilde" for vile. Though some modern texts set the Fl (or alternative Q) setting, others modernise. Fl will be set as is with no annotation.

ALTERNATIVE SETTINGS OF A WORD WHERE DIFFERENT SPELLINGS SUGGEST DIFFERENT MEANINGS

Far more complicated is the situation where, while an Elizabethan could substitute one word formation for another and still imply the same thing, to modern eyes the substituted word has an entirely different meaning to the one it has replaced. The following is by no means an exclusive list of the more common dual-spelling, dual-meaning words

anticke-antique	mad-made	sprite-spirit
born-borne	metal-mettle	sun-sonne
hart-heart	mote-moth	travel-travaill
human-humane	pour-(po wre)-power	through-thorough
lest-least	reverent-reverend	troth-truth
lose-loose	right-rite	whether-whither

Some of these doubles offer a metrical problem too, for example "sprite," a one syllable word, versus "spirit." A potential problem occurs in *A Midsummer Nights Dream,* where the modern text s set Q1's "thorough," and thus the scansion pattern of elegant magic can be established, whereas F1's more plebeian "through" sets up a much more awkward and clumsy moment.

The F reading will be set in the Folio Text, as will the modern texts' substitution of a different word formation in the Modern Text. If the modern text substitution has the potential to alter the meaning (and sometimes scansion) of the line, it will be noted accordingly.

PART TWO: WORD FORMATIONS COUNTED AS EQUIVALENTS FOR THE FOLLOWING SPEECHES

Often the spelling differences between the original and modern texts are quite obvious, as with "she"/"shee". And sometimes Folio text passages are so flooded with longer (and sometimes shorter) spellings that, as described in the General Introduction, it would seem that vocally something unusual is taking place as the character speaks.

However, there are some words where the spelling differences are so marginal that they need not be explored any further. The following is by no mean s an exclusive list of word s that in the main will not be taken into account when discussing emotional moments in the various commentaries accompanying the audition speeches.

(modern text spelling shown first)

and - &	murder - murther	tabor - taber
apparent - apparant	mutinous - mutenous	ta'en - tane
briars - briers	naught - nought	then - than
choice - choise	obey - obay	theater - theatre
defense - defence	o'er - o're	uncurrant - uncurrent
debtor - debter	offense - offence	than - then
enchant - inchant	quaint - queint	venomous - venemous
endurance - indurance	reside - recide	virtue - vertue
ere - e'er	Saint - S.	weight - waight
expense - expence	sense - sence	
has - ha's	sepulchre - sepulcher	
heinous - hainous	show - shew	
1'11 - Ile	solicitor - soliciter	
increase - encrease	sugar - suger	

APPENDIX 3:
THE PATTERN OF MAGIC, RITUAL &
INCANTATION

THE PATTERNS OF "NORMAL" CONVERSATION

The normal pattern of a regular Shakespearean verse line is akin to five pairs of human heart beats, with ten syllables being arranged in five pairs of beats, each pair alternating a pattern of a weak stress followed by a strong stress. Thus, a normal ten syllable heartbeat line (with the emphasis on the capitalised words) would read as

weak- STRONG, weak - STRONG, weak- STRONG, weak- STRONG, weak- STRONG
(shall   I   com-   PARE thee   TO   a   SUMM- ers DAY)

Breaks would either be in length (under or over ten syllables) or in rhythm (any combinations of stresses other than the five pairs of weak-strong as shown above), or both together.

THE PATTERNS OF MAGIC, RITUAL, AND INCANTATION

Whenever magic is used in the Shakespeare plays the form of the spoken verse changes markedly in two ways . The length is usually reduced from ten to just seven syllables, and the pattern of stresses is completely reversed, as if the heartbeat was being forced either by the circumstances of the scene or by the need of the speaker to completely change direction. Thus in comparison to the normal line shown above, or even the occasional minor break, the more tortured and even dangerous magic or ritual line would read as

STRONG - weak, STRONG- weak, STRONG - weak, STRONG
(WHEN   shall   WE   three   MEET   a   GAINE)

The strain would be even more severely felt in an extended passage, as when the three weyward Sisters begin the potion that will fetch Macbeth to them. Again, the spoken emphasis is on the capitalised words and the effort of, and/or fixed determination in, speaking can clearly be felt.

> THRICE the BRINDed CAT hath MEW"D
> THRICE and ONCE the HEDGE-Pigge WHIN"D
> HARPier CRIES, 'tis TIME, 'tis TIME.

UNUSUAL ASPECTS OF MAGIC

It's not always easy for the characters to maintain it. And the magic doesn't always come when the character expects it. What is even more interesting is that while the pattern is found a lot in the Comedies, it is usually in much gentler situations, often in songs *(Two Gentlemen of Verona, Merry Wives of Windsor, Much Ado About Nothing, Twelfth Night, The Winters Tale)* and/or simplistic poetry *(Loves Labours Lost* and *As You Like It)*, as well as the casket sequence in *The Merchant of Venice.*

It's too easy to dismiss these settings as inferior poetry known as doggerel. But this may be doing the moment and the character a great disservice. The language may be simplistic, but the passion and the magical/ritual intent behind it is wonderfully sincere. It's not just a matter of magic for the sake of magic, as with Pucke and Oberon enchanting mortals and Titania. It's a matter of the human heart's desires too. Orlando, in *As You Like It,* when writing peons of praise to Rosalind suggesting that she is composed of the best parts of the mythical heroines because

> THEREfore HEAVen NATure CHARG"D
> THAT one B0Die SHOULD be FILL"D
> WITH all GRACes WIDE enLARG"D

And what could be better than Autolycus *(The Winters Tale)* using magic in his opening song as an extra enticement to trap the unwary into buying all his peddler's goods, ballads, and trinkets.

To help the reader, most magic/ritual lines will be bolded in the Folio text version of the speeches.

ACKNOWLEDGMENTS

Neil dedicated *The Applause First Folio in Modern Type*
"To All Who Have Gone Before"
and there are so many who have gone before in the sharing of Shakespeare through publication. Back to John Heminge and Henry Condell who published *Mr. William Shakespeares Comedies, Histories, & Tragedies* which we now know as The First Folio and so preserved 18 plays of Shakespeare which might otherwise have been lost. As they wrote in their note "To the great Variety of Readers.":

> Reade him, therefore; and againe, and againe : And if then you doe not like him, surely you are in some manifest danger, not to understand him. And so we leave you to other of his Friends, whom if you need, can be your guides: if you neede them not, you can lead yourselves, and others, and such readers we wish him.

I want to thank John Cerullo for believing in these books and helping to spread Neil's vision. I want to thank Rachel Reiss for her invaluable advice and assistance. I want to thank my wife, Maren and my family for giving me support, but above all I want to thank Julie Stockton, Neil's widow, who was able to retrive Neil's files from his old non-internet connected Mac, without which these books would not be possible. Thank you Julie.
Shakespeare for Everyone!

Paul Sugarman, April 2021

AUTHOR BIOS

Neil Freeman (1941-2015) trained as an actor at the Bristol Old Vic Theatre School. In the world of professional Shakespeare he acted in fourteen of the plays, directed twenty-four, and coached them all many times over.

His groundbreaking work in using the first printings of the Shakespeare texts in performance, on the rehearsal floor and in the classroom led to lectures at the Shakespeare Association of America and workshops at both the ATHE and VASTA, and grants/fellowships from the National Endowment for the Arts (USA), The Social Science and Humanities Research Council (Canada), and York University in Toronto. He prepared and annotated the thirty-six individual Applause First Folio editions of Shakespeare's plays and the complete *The Applause First Folio of Shakespeare in Modern Type*. For Applause he also compiled *Once More Unto the Speech, Dear Friends*, three volumes (Comedy, History and Tragedy) of Shakespeare speeches with commentary and insights to inform audition preparation.

He was Professor Emeritus in the Department of Theatre, Film and Creative Writing at the University of British Columbia, and dramaturg with The Savage God project, both in Vancouver, Canada. He also taught regularly at the National Theatre School of Canada, Concordia University, Brigham Young University.. He had a Founder's Ring (and the position of Master Teacher) with Shakespeare & Company in Lenox, Mass: he was associated with the Will Geer Theatre in Los Angeles; Bard on the Beach in Vancouver; Repercussion Theatre in Montreal; and worked with the Stratford Festival, Canada, and Shakespeare Santa Cruz.

Paul Sugarman is an actor, editor, writer, and teacher of Shakespeare. He is founder of the Instant Shakespeare Company, which has presented annual readings of all of Shakespeare's plays in New York City for over twenty years. For Applause Theatre & Cinema Books, he edited John Russell Brown's publication of *Shakescenes: Shakespeare for Two* and The Applause Shakespeare Library, as well as Neil Freeman's Applause First Folio Editions and *The Applause First Folio of Shakespeare in Modern Type*. He has published pocket editions of all of Shakespeare's plays using the original settings of the First Folio in modern type for Puck Press. Sugarman studied with Kristin Linklater and Tina Packer at Shakespeare & Company where he met Neil Freeman.

CPSIA information can be obtained
at www.ICGtesting.com
Printed in the USA
LVHW012024130622
721185LV00004B/330

9 781493 056842